CAST

IN ORDER OF APPEARANCE

Belvile, *a Colonel*	*four come out*	Hugh Quarshie
Frederick, *his friend*	*of England*	Peter Guinness
Blunt, *a country gull*		David Troughton
Willmore, *the Rover*		Jeremy Irons
Lucetta, *a whore*		Vivienne Rochester
Sancho, *her man*		Tony Armatrading
Florinda	*three sisters*	Geraldine Fitzgerald
Valeria		Susie Fairfax
Hellena		Imogen Stubbs
Don Pedro, *their brother*		Norman Eshley
Stephano	*his servants*	Trevor Gordon
Callis		Jenni George
Angellica Bianca, *a famous courtesan*		Stephanie Beacham
Moretta, *her woman*		Rosalind Boxall
Sebastian	*her bravos*	Togo Igawa
Biskey		Patrick Robinson
Don Antonio, *the Viceroy's son*		Philip Sully
Diego, *his servant*		Stan Pretty
Phillip, *servant to the English*		Brian Lawson
Masquers/servants		Tony Armatrading
		Trevor Gordon
		Togo Igawa
		Stan Pretty
		Patrick Robinson
		Vivian Rochester

Directed by	**John Barton**
Designed by	**Louise Belson**
Lighting by	**Wayne Dowdeswell** and **Geraint Pughe**
Music by	**Guy Woolfenden**
Musical Director	**Jonathan Rutherford**
Company voice work by	**Cicely Berry** and **Patsy Rodenburg**
Assistant Director	**Leona Heimfeld**
Stage Manager	**Michael Townsend**
Deputy Stage Manager	**Kate Trevers**

MUSICIANS

Jonathan Rutherford	**Keyboards**
Colin Ray	**Trumpet**
Tony McVey/Bernard Shaw	**Percussion**

This performance is approximately 2 hours 45 minutes long including one interval of 20 minutes.
First performance of this RSC production, Swan Theatre, Stratford-upon-Avon, 3 July 1986
Mermaid Theatre, London, 4 November 1987
Please do not smoke or use cameras or tape recorders in the auditorium. And please remember that noise such as whispering, coughing, rustling programmes and the bleeping of digital watches can be distracting to performers and also spoils the performance for other members of the audience.

Biographies

TONY ARMATRADING *Sancho*
Theatre: Male Nurse in *Whose Life Is It Anyway?* (Birmingham & Coventry), *Antigone, Cinderella,* Telephone Man in *Barefoot In The Park, Joseph And The Amazing Technicolour Dreamcoat* (Croydon), Jelly Roll Morton in *Jelly Roll Soul* (Deptford Albany and tour), *Smile Orange, Hansel And Gretel, Moon On A Rainbow* (Stratford East), *Measure For Measure* (NT).
RSC: Sancho in *The Rover.* This season: Joffer/Second Captain in *The Fair Maid Of The West,* Scipio in *The Great White Hope,* Tybalt in *Romeo and Juliet.*
Television: *Angels, Grange Hill, Empire Road, Alive and Kicking, A Taste Of Honey, Cats Eyes, Let's Pretend.*
Radio: *Some Kind Of Hero, The Wasted Years.*

JOHN BARTON *Director*
Theatre: Includes *The School For Scandal* (Haymarket), *Waste* (Lyric Theatre).
RSC: An Associate Director of the RSC. Devised *The Hollow Crown* and *The Art of Seduction.* Co-directed the Stratford Histories cycle with Peter Hall, edited the text of *The War of the Roses.* Co-directed *Henry IV Parts 1 and 2.* Directed: *Love's Labour's Lost, Julius Caesar, Troilus and Cressida, Twelfth Night, Measure for Measure, The Tempest, Othello, When Thou Art King, Henry V, Richard II, King John, Cymbeline, Much Ado About Nothing, The Winter's Tale, King Lear, Doctor Faustus, Perkin Warbeck, Pillars of the Community, A Midsummer Night's Dream, The Way of the World, The Merchant of Venice, The Greeks, Hamlet, Titus Andronicus/Two Gentlemen of Verona, La Ronde, Life's A Dream, The Devils, Waste, Dreamplay, The Rover.*
Television: *The Morte d'Arthur, Playing Shakespeare.*

STEPHANIE BEACHAM *Angellica Bianca*
Theatre: Includes: Lady Mortimer in *Henry IV,* Clarice in *Servant of Two Masters,* Marigold in *Toad of Toad Hall,* First Witch in *Macbeth* (Liverpool Everyman), *Monsieur Barnett* (Bristol Old Vic), Irma in *Mad Woman of Chaillot,* Louka in *Arms and the Man, The Silent Woman, Gaslight* (Oxford Playhouse), *The Basement, Tea Party* (Duchess Theatre), Ruth in *The Homecoming,* Juno in *The Tempest,* Nora in *A Dolls House* (Nottingham Playhouse), Helen in *On Approval* (Haymarket Theatre), Helen in *Absurd Person Singular* (Sheffield, Crucible), *The Singular Life of Albert Nobbs* (New End Theatre), *London Cuckold* (Royal Court), *Can You Hear Me At The Back* (Piccadilly Theatre), *Terra Nova* (Palace Theatre, Watford), *Happy Families* (Duke of York's Theatre), *Twelfth Night* (British Council), *Venice Preserv'd* (NT).
RSC: Angellica Bianca in *The Rover.*
Television: *The Picnic, The Silent Preacher, Ego Hugo, All The World's A Stage, Tenko, Inside Television, Sorrell & Son, Give Us A Clue, Connie, The Colbys, Napoleon and Josephine.* **Radio:** *Handful of Dust.*
Films: *The Games, Tam Lyn, The Nightcomers, Movie Blackmail, Fengriffen, And Now The Screaming Starts, The Confessional, Inseminoid.*

LOUISE BELSON *Designer*
Trained at Wimbledon School of Art.
Theatre: Was resident and associate designer at Crucible Theatre Sheffield for several seasons. Has also designed for Soho Poly, Birmingham Rep, Wild Cat Co. Glasgow, Bristol Express, All Change Art Community Theatre, Young Vic.
RSC: *Dreamplay* (costumes only), *The Rover.*
Television: Programmes for Channel Four.

ROSALIND BOXALL *Moretta*
Theatre: Seasons at Colchester, Nottingham and Birmingham. Ophelia in *Hamlet,,* Desdemona in *Othello,* Margaret in *Henry VI Parts 1, 2 and 3,* Natalia Petrovna in *A Month in the country,* The Witch in *The Tinder Box* (Repertory). Lady Bracknell in *The Importance of Being Earnest,* Laura in *The Father,* Countess in *All's Well that Ends Well,* Lady Markby in *The Ideal Husband,* Mrs Dudgeon in *The Devil's Disciple* (Birmingham). Jacquenetta in *Love's Labour's Lost* (Old Vic), The Bride in *Blood Wedding* (Arts Theatre), Nurse in *Romeo and Juliet,* Miss Prism in *The Importance of Being Earnest,* Emilia in *Othello* (Young Vic). Mrs Tarleton in *Misalliance,* Mrs Carghill in *Elder Statesman* (Malvern Festival), Mrs Winslow in *The Winslow Boy* (UK tour), Lady Bountiful in *The Beaux' Stratagem* (Cambridge Theatre Company), Gertrude in *Hamlet,* Berinthia in *The Relapse* (Australian tour).
RSC: First Queen in *The Two Noble Kinsmen,* Moretta in *The Rover,* Duchess of York in *Richard II,* Antonia in *Worlds Apart,* Gentlewoman in *Macbeth.* Aphra Behn in *Close Encounters of the Swan Kind* (RSC Festival), Mrs Violet Layden in *They Shoot Horses Don't They?*
Television: *Age of Hypocrisy, Don't Be Silly, Juliet Bravo, Muck and Brass.*

WAYNE DOWDESWELL *Lighting Designer*
Theatre: *The Fantasticks, Salad Days,* Verdi's *Macbeth, Nabucco* and *Aida,* Mozart's *Cosi Fan Tutte, Don Giovanni* (Sheffield University Theatre), *No More Sitting On The Old School Bench, Painted Veg and Parkinson, Fanshen Hunchback of Notre Dame* (Manchester Contact Theatre).
RSC: Joined the RSC in 1978. Worked at TOP as Deputy Electrician and the Electrician. TOP productions include *Money, Golden Girls, Desert Air, Today, The Dillen, Mary After the Queen, The Quest.* Currently Resident Lighting Designer at the Swan Theatre where his productions include *The Two Noble Kinsmen, Every Man In His Humour, The Rover* and *The Fair Maid of the West.*

NORMAN ESHLEY *Don Pedro*
Theatre: Includes *Measure for Measure, Hamlet, Romeo and Juliet* (Bristol Old Vic Touring Company), *Early Morning, Twelfth Night* (Royal Court Theatre), *Vivat Vivat Regina* (Chichester & West End), *Sergius Saranoff in Arms And The Man, Same Time Next Year, Grass Is Greener, Lady Chatterley's Lover* (National Tour), *Heartbreak House, La Ronde, Soul Of The White Ant* (Manchester Royal Exchange), *The Importance Of Being Earnest* (Birmingham Rep), *Jubilee* (Yvonne Arnaud Theatre), *The Exorcism* (National Tour), *Way Upstream* (Yvonne Arnaud Theatre & Tour), lead role in *Romantic Comedy* (The Mill at Sonning).
RSC: Don Pedro in *The Rover*
Television: *Canterbury Tales, Warship ,Sweeney, Professionals, Maybury, The Outsider, I Claudius, Onedin Line, Man About The House, George and Mildred, Duchess of Duke Street, The Bouncing Boy, Fat, Love Story, Man Of Our Times, The Tell Tale Heart, Hilary, The Black Tower, Brookside, Executive Stress, Late Expectations, Minder.*
Films: *The Immortal Story, Blind Terror, House of Mortal Sin.*

SUSIE FAIRFAX *Valeria*
Theatre: Seasons at Plymouth, Coventry. Toine in *Piaf,* Thelma Sparrow in *Birdbath,* Mrs Dai Bread/Rosie Probert in *Under Milkwood,* Liddy Smallbury in *Far from the Madding Crowd,* Nerissa in *The Merchant of Venice, Pygmalion, Equus, Devonshire Cream* (Repertory). The Woman in *After Liverpool* (Soho Poly). *Roots, The Devil's Disciple, The Royal Pardon* (UK tours).

RSC
Mermaid Theatre

Sponsored by
Royal Insurance

EDDIE KULUKUNDIS
by arrangement with Frank and Woji Gero and Playhouse Productions
presents
an adaptation of

THE ROVER

by Aphra Behn

(The Banished Cavaliers)

A programme/text with commentary by Simon Trussler

Contents

Swan Theatre Plays published by Methuen London
by arrangement with the Royal Shakespeare Company

methuen

Sponsored by
Royal Insurance

The Royal Shakespeare Company (RSC), is the title under which the Royal Shakespeare Theatre, Stratford-upon-Avon, has operated since 1961. Now one of the best-known theatre companies in the world, the RSC builds on a long and distinguished history of theatre in Stratford-upon-Avon.

In essence, the aim of the Company is the same as that expressed in 1905 by Sir Frank Benson, then director of the Stratford theatre: 'to train a company, every member of which would be an essential part of a homogenous whole, consecrated to the practice of the dramatic arts and especially to the representation of the plays of Shakespeare'. The RSC is formed around a core of associate artists – actors, directors, designers and others – with the aim that their different skills should combine, over the years, to produce a distinctive approach to theatre, both classical and modern.

When, just a year after the granting, in 1925, of its Royal Charter, the theatre was almost completely destroyed by fire, a worldwide campaign was launched to build a new one. Productions moved to a local cinema until the new theatre, designed by Elisabeth Scott, was opened by the Prince of Wales on 23 April, 1932. Over the next thirty years, under the influence of directors such as Robert Atkins, Bridges-Adams, Iden Payne, Komisarjevsky, Sir Barry Jackson, Glen Byam Shaw and Anthony Quayle, the Shakespeare Memorial Theatre maintained a worldwide reputation.

In 1960, the newly appointed artistic director, Peter Hall, extended the re-named Royal Shakespeare Company's operations to include a London base at the Aldwych Theatre, and widened the Company's repertoire to include modern as well as classical work. Other innovations of the period which have shaped today's Company were the travelling Theatregoround and experimental work which included the Theatre of Cruelty season.

Under Trevor Nunn, who took over as artistic director in 1968, this experimental work in small performances spaces led, in 1974, to the opening of The Other Place, Stratford-upon-Avon. This was a rehearsal space converted into a theatre and in 1977 its London counterpart, The Warehouse, opened with a policy of presenting new British plays. In the same year the RSC played its first season in Newcastle upon Tyne – now an annual event. In 1978, the year in which Terry Hands joined Trevor Nunn as artistic director, the RSC also fulfilled an ambition to tour towns and villages with little or no access to live professional theatre.

In 1982, the RSC moved its London base to the Barbican Centre in the City of London, opening both the Barbican Theatre, specially built for the RSC by the generosity of the Corporation of the City of London, and The Pit, a small theatre converted like The Warehouse and The Other Place, from a rehearsal room.

Last season saw the opening of a new, fifth RSC theatre: the Swan Theatre in Stratford-upon-Avon. Built within the section of the shell of the original Shakespeare Memorial Theatre which escaped the 1926 fire, the Swan is a Jacobean-style playhouse staging the once hugely popular but now rarely-seen plays of Shakespeare's contemporaries during the period 1570-1750. This new dimension to the Royal Shakespeare Company's work has been made possible by the extremely generous gift of a benefactor, Frederick R. Koch. In March 1987 the RSC, supported by Frank and Woji Gero and Playhouse Productions – and, more recently, by Eddie Kulukundis – presented a season at the Mermaid Theatre which included productions from the 1986 Swan season.

In early 1987 Terry Hands became sole Artistic Director and Chief Executive of the Company.

Throughout its history, the RSC has augmented its central operations with national and international tours, films, television programmes, commercial transfers and fringe activities. It has won over 200 national and international awards in its 25 years, including most recently the Queen's Award for Export – but despite box office figures which, it is thought, have no equal anywhere in the world, the costs of RSC activities cannot be recouped from ticket sales alone. We rely on assistance from the Arts Council of Great Britain, amounting to about 40% of our costs in any one year, from work in other media and, increasingly, from commercial sponsorship. To find out more about the RSC's activities and to make sure of priority booking for our productions, why not become a member of the Company's Mailing List. Details of how to apply can be found in the theatre foyer.

RSC: Lady in *The Winter's Tale*, Tib in *Every Man in His Humour*, Valeria in *The Rover*, Glasha in *The Storm*, Hope in *Sarcophagus*.
Television: *Winter Sunshine*, *Partners in Crime – Agatha Christie*, *My Cousin Rachel*, *Reilly – Ace of Spies*, *Fame is the Spur*, *Stalky and Co*, *Bognor*, *God Speed Co-operation*, *Nanny*, *Adelaide Bartlett – A Question of Guilt*. **Film:** *Winter Flight*, *Tarka the Otter*.

GERALDINE FITZGERALD *Florinda*
Theatre: *Sweet Charity*, Janeen in *Leave Him to Heaven*, Miriam in *Happy End*, Clara in *The Vortex*, Patti in *Season's Greetings* (Manchester Library Theatre), Maisie in *The Boyfriend* (Belgrade, Coventry). Jane in *Steaming* (Comedy Theatre), *The Taming of the Shrew* (Stratford East), Princess Ba-Ba in *A Night in Old Peking*, *Dracula* (Lyric, Hammersmith), *Saki* (Gate, Notting Hill). *Godspell*, Lady Cynthia Muldoon in *The Real Inspector Hound* (UK tours), Magenta in *The Rocky Horror Show* (European tour).
RSC: Rose in *Flight*, Florinda in *The Rover*, Luisa in *Worlds Apart*, Dr Anna Petrovna in *Sarcophagus*, Jackie Miller in *They Shoot Horses Don't They?*, *Lynchville* (RSC Festival).

JENNI GEORGE *Callis*
Theatre: Seasons at Ipswich, Royal Exchange, Manchester, Leatherhead and Leeds. Maria in *Twelfth Night*, Sarah in *The Lover*, Frenchy in *Grease*, The Girl in *Hello Out There*, Adriana in *The Comedy of Errors*, *Cymbeline*, *Great Expectations*, *The Admirable Crichton*, Josephine Baker in *Piaf*, A *Midsummer Night's Dream* (Repertory). Alea in *Split Second* (Lyric, Hammersmith). *Getting Plenty* (Temba Theatre Company UK tour).
RSC: Lady in *Romeo and Juliet*, Second Queen in *The Two Noble Kinsmen*, Callis in *The Rover*, Queen Tota in *The Fair Maid of the West*.
Television: *Jury*, *Just Good Friends*, *Johnny Jarvis*, *The Frontline*.

TREVOR GORDON *Stephano*
Theatre: *It's a Woman's Place*, *The Nail Makers* (Birmingham), *The Mark Twain Show*, *Wheels*, *Injury Time*, *In Need of Care*, *Puzzles*, *Frankie's Friends*, *Billy the Kid*, *Breaking Chains*, *The Zulu Hut Club*, *Hidden Meanings* (London). *Marathon Madness*, *Chairperson*, *Peace Maker* (UK tours).
RSC: Zach in *The Blood Knot*, *Ogun Abibiman* (RSC Festival). Pastoral Servant in *The Winter's Tale*, Stephano in *The Rover*. This Season: Stanley in *Flight*, Drawer/Sailor/Spanish Prisoner in *The Fair Maid of the West*. Armand in *The Balcony*, Deacon in *The Great White Hope*.
Television: *Empire Road*, *Buccaneer*, *Angels*.
Film: *Management of Discipline* (local government training film).

PETER GUINNESS *Frederick*
Theatre: Seasons at Dundee, Southampton, Manchester. Includes Sam in *The Homecoming*, Sgt Kite in *The Recruiting Officer*, Ariel in *The Tempest* (Repertory). The Nantuckian in *Moby Dick* (Royal Exchange, Manchester), Tybalt in *Romeo and Juliet* (Old Vic, Bristol), De Flores in *The Changeling* (Contact Theatre, Manchester). Aston in *The Caretaker* (Greenwich), Edgar in *King Lear*, Hamlet in *Hamlet, the First Quarto* (Orange Tree Theatre). The Duke in *Measure for Measure* (Young Vic). Workshops for the New Shakespeare Company (Round House and Mermaid).
RSC: Gideon Sachs in *Flight*, Theseus in *The Two Noble Kinsmen*, Frederick in *The Rover*, Macduff in *Macbeth*, The Investigator in *Sarcophagus*, James Reilly in *They Shoot Horses Don't They*.
Television: Includes *Hazell*, *Sister Dora*, *Keep Smiling*, *The Legend of King Arthur*, *The Brack Report*, *I Remember Nelson*, *Squadron*, *Smiley's People*, *By The Sword Divided*, *Hounds of Love*.
Film: *The Keep*, *Family Ties*, *American Roulette*. **Radio:** *Fame is the Spur*.

LEONA HEIMFELD *Assistant Director*
Theatre: Founder Member and Director of Criminal Acts Theatre Co, Assistant Director in Rehearsal Readings of *Up to the Sun...*, and *Passion in Six Days* (Royal Court Theatre Upstairs), *Cargo Cult* (Cafe Theatre Upstairs). **RSC:** Directed and adapted *Aphra Behn* (RSC Youth Festival), *Cargo Cult* (Early Stages). Assistant director on *The Rover*.

TOGO IGAWA *Sebastian*
Theatre: Member of the Black Tent Theatre, Tokyo (1969-82) performing in over one hundred cities throughout Japan.
RSC: Sebastian in *The Rover*, Alcade in *The Fair Maid of the West*. Teddy/Leaker in *The Silver King* (RSC Festival), Doctor in *They Shoot Horses Don't They?*, El Jefe/French Handler in *The Great White Hope*.
Television: *Gems*. **Films:** *The Man Who Shot Christmas*, *Half Moon Street*.
Radio: *Hiroshima: The Movie*, *This is the Age of the Train*.

JEREMY IRONS *Willmore*
Theatre: Seasons at Bristol Old Vic including Florizel in *The Winter's Tale*, Simon in *Hay Fever*, Nick in *What the Butler Saw*, Don Pedro in *Much Ado About Nothing*, Nick in *The Caretaker* (Young Vic), John the Baptist in *Godspell*, Jameson in *The Rear Column* (London), Petruchio in *The Taming of the Shrew* (New Shakespeare Co), Henry in *The Real Thing* (Broadway).
RSC: Harry Thunder in *Wild Oats*, Leontes in *The Winter's Tale*, Willmore in *The Rover*, title role in *Richard II*.
Television: Includes *Love for Lydia*, *Langrishe Go Down*, *Brideshead Revisited*, *The Captain's Doll*.
Film: *Nijinsky*, *The French Lieutenant's Woman*, *Moonlighting*, *Betrayal*, *The Wild Duck*, *Swann in Love*, *The Mission*, *My Fair Lady*, recording and concert at Royal Albert Hall.

BRIAN LAWSON *Phillip*
Theatre: Seasons at York, Ipswich, Newcastle, Canterbury, Birmingham. Edmund Kean in *Kean*, Dysart in *Equus*, Chauvelin in *The Scarlet Pimpernel*, Ramble in *Lock Up Your Daughters*, Truffaldino in *Servant Of Two Masters* (Repertory). Gratiano in *The Merchant Of Venice*, Jan in *Miss Julie*, Arthur Henderson in *After The Rain* (Birmingham). Nestor/Oscar in *Irma La Douce* (Ipswich), Ellyot Chase in *Private Lives*, Bluntschli in *Arms And The Man* (Nairobi). Alan Baker in *Come Blow Your Horn* (London). Tallon in *The Changing Room* (Royal Court). Cromwell in *A Man For All Seasons*, Narrator in *Side By Side By Sondheim* (UK tours). *Birds On The Wing* (Canada).
RSC: Apothecary in *Romeo and Juliet*, Gentleman in *The Winter's Tale*, Phillip in *The Rover*, First Captain/Alderman/Spanish Captain in *The Fair Maid of the West*. Directed *The Silver King* (RSC Festival).
Television: *Z Cars*, *New Scotland Yard*, *Crown Court*, *Coronation Street*, *Big Deal*. **Film:** *O Lucky Man*, *Tell It Like It Is*.
Directing: Artistic Director, St Andrew's Rep (1973-78), Associate Director, Classic Stage Co, New York City (1981-82), Guest Director, Theatre By The Grove, Indiana, Pennsylvania.
Writing: *Lucifer in Starlight* (stage play), episodes of *The Bluffers* (US TV).
Other: Fight director/combat instructor for theatre, films, television, in numerous productions over more than 25 years.

STAN PRETTY *Diego*
Theatre: Goldberg in *The Birthday Party* (Glasgow Citizens and tour), Klein in *Arsenic and Old Lace*, Digger in *The Hasty Heart* (Windsor). Judge and Washerwoman in *Toad of Toad Hall*, Reuben in *Joseph And The Amazing Technicolour Dreamcoat*, Rooney in *Arsenic and Old Lace*, Lord

Broadcasting: London Arts correspondent for Australian Broadcasting Cantelupe in *Waste* (London), Snout in *A Midsummer Night's Dream*, Sea Captain/Priest in *Twelfth Night* (Regent's Park), *Travelling North*, *The Wild Duck* (Lyric Hammersmith), *Julius Caesar* (UK tour).
RSC: Escalus' Aide in *Romeo and Juliet*, Diego in *The Rover*, Willoughby in *Richard II*, Caithness in *Macbeth*. Jaikes in *The Silver King*, title role in *The Shop Assistant* (RSC Festival), Louis in *The Balcony*.
Television: *Minder, Bergerac, Partners in Crime, Dempsey and Makepeace, Rumpole of the Bailey, Jenny's War, On the Line*, various children's programmes, presenter of NHS training films.
Corporation.
Writing: Theatre correspondent for *London Outlook* (New York).

HUGH QUARSHIE *Belvile*
Theatre: *Blackball Game* (Sheffield and London), *On The Out, Whose Life Is It Anyway?* (London). Posthumus/Cloten in *Cymberline*, title role in *The Admirable Crichton* (Royal Exchange, Manchester), Val in *Split Second* (Lyric, Hammersmith), Jack Jefferson in *The Great White Hope* (Tricycle Theatre).
RSC: Outlaw in *The Two Gentlemen of Verona*, Aaron in *Titus Andronicus*, Cleomenes in *The Winter's Tale*, Hotspur in *Henry IV*, Tybalt in *Romeo and Juliet*, Arcite in *The Two Noble Kinsmen*, Belvile in *The Rover*, Banquo in *Macbeth*, Jack Jefferson in *The Great White Hope*.
Television: *The Knowledge, The Jail Diary of Albie Sachs, A Midsummer Night's Dream, Buccaneer, Wolcott, Rumpole of the Bailey, Wide Games, Angels, Titus Andronicus, Drums Along Balmoral Drive*.
Film: *The Dogs of War, Baby – Secret of the Lost Legend, Highlander*.
Radio: Broadcasts for Radio 4, BBC African Service, *Afternoon Theatre*.

PATRICK ROBINSON *Biskey*
RSC: First engagement since leaving LAMDA. Bluey in *Peacemaker*, Snatch in *Class Enemy* (RSC Festival), Pastoral Servant in *The Winter's Tale*, Biskey in *The Rover*. This season: Seyton in *Macbeth*, Policeman in *Romeo and Juliet*, Rollo in *They Shoot Horses Don't They?*, Rudy in *The Great White Hope*.

VIVIENNE ROCHESTER *Lucetta*
Theatre: Yvonne and other roles in *A Mouthful of Birds* (Royal Court), Winnie in *Blues for Railton* (Albany Empire), Miss Branden in *Smile Orange* (Theatre Royal Stratford), Judy in *Money To Live* (Theatre Upstairs, Royal Court), Pirates Princess in *Marma B* (Arts Theatre), UK tour with Joint Stock (1986) and Black Theatre Co-operative (1984).
RSC: This season: The Thief in *The Balcony*, Lady in *Romeo And Juliet*, Sister in *The Great White Hope*, Lucetta in *The Rover*.
Television: *Gentle Touch, Late Starter, Streets Ahead, Killing Time, Some Drinks And Good Times, Take Back What's Yours, Basin*.
Radio: *Ascension Ritual, Killing Time, Fancy You Minding That*.

JONATHAN RUTHERFORD *Musical Director*
Theatre: Children's music coach for Annie (West End and UK tour). Assistant Musical Director for *John Curry's Theatre of Skating 2, The Sound of Music, The Ratepayer's Iolanthe* (London).
RSC: Music Director for *Poppy* (West End), *Hamlet, Richard II, The Rover*. Keyboards for *Les Liaisons*.
Compositions: include *The Star Child in Solitude Op 9* – cantata based on three act chamber opera *Star Child*; settings of groups of poems by EE Cumings; *The Whole Garden Will Bow* for baritone and piano; *All Skies Fall* for tenor and piano; *O Sweet Spontaneous Earth* for unaccompanied soprano; setting of *Psalm 13* for chorus and string orchestra; *The Pied Piper*

for narrator and nine wind instruments; *Clarinet Quintet in A major* written for amateur musicians; *Sonata quasi Fantasia* for unaccompanied violin; *Prayers to St Cecilia* and a one act opera *The Nightingale and the Rose*.

IMOGEN STUBBS *Hellena*
Theatre: Sally Bowles in *Cabaret*, Polly in *The Boyfriend* (Ipswich).
RSC: Gaoler's Daughter in *The Two Noble Kinsmen*, Hellena in *The Rover*, Queen Isabel in *Richard II*.
Television: *The Browning Version, Granville Jones*.
Film: *Nanou, The Apple Tree*.

PHILIP SULLY *Don Antonio*
Theatre: Seasons at Perth, Ipswich, Worcester, Derby, Birmingham, Ludlow. Joseph Surface in *The School for Scandal*, Mercutio in *Romeo and Juliet*, Oliver in *As You Like It*, The Interrogator in *The Prisoner*, Joey in *In Praise of Love* (Repertory). Gratiano in *The Merchant of Venice*, Mordred in *Lancelot and Guinevere*, Angus in *Macbeth* (Old Vic), German Mercenary in *Lorenzaccio* (NT). Orsino in *Twelfth Night*, Tybalt in *Romeo and Juliet*, Hotspur in *Henry IV Part 1*, Banquo in *Macbeth* (UK tours).
RSC: Balthasar in *Romeo and Juliet*, Artesius in *The Two Noble Kinsmen*, Don Antonio in *The Rover*, Carrol in *The Fair Maid of the West*. Victor Frankenstein in Frankenstein, Gaveston/Mephistopheles in *Marlowe*.
Television: *Standing in for Henry*.
Radio: *Moby Dick, Eugene Onegin, Troilus and Cressida, Cymberline, Emperor*.

DAVID TROUGHTON *Blunt*
Theatre: Seasons at Arts Theatre and Leeds Playhouse. Knocker White in *The Wedding Feast, No More Sitting on the Old School Bench* (Leeds), Evans in *Terra Nova* (Watford), *The Case of the Frightened Lady* (Bromley). Martin in *Fool for Love*, Peter in *Don Juan*, Serjeant Musgrave's Dance (NT). Hal in *Loot* (Royal Court).
RSC: Ross in *Macbeth*, Conrad in *Much Ado About Nothing*, Aslak in *Peer Gynt*, Bouton in *Molière*, Clown in *Antony and Cleopatra*, Sebastian in *The Roaring Girl*, Cob in *Every Man In His Humour*, Blunt in *The Rover*, Porter in *Macbeth*.
Television: Includes *David Copperfield, Chips with Everything, Our Mutual Friend, The Norman Conquests, Wings, Man of Destiny, Hi-De-Hi, Sorry, Angels, A Very Peculiar Practice*.
Film: *Dance With A Stranger, The Chain*. **Radio:** *Psmith*.

GUY WOOLFENDEN *Composer*
Theatre: Head of Music for the RSC, for whom he has composed more than 150 scores. Music for productions at the Comedie Francaise, Burgtheater, Teatro di Stabile and Den Nationale Scene, Bergen. Artistic Director for the Cambridge Festival.
Films and Television: *The Chester Mystery Plays, Macbeth, Antony and Cleopatra, The Comedy of Errors, Work is a Four Letter Word, The Various Ends of Mrs F's Friends, Secrets, Playing Shakespeare, What A Way To Run A Revolution, Heart Of The Country*.
Ballet: Composed and arranged *Anna Karenina, Three Musketeers* for Australian Ballet.
Conducting: Three productions for Scottish Opera. First UK performances of Nielsen's *Saul and David*, Tchaikovsky's *The Maid of Orleans* and Liszt's *Dion Sanche*. Concerts with major symphony orchestras in the UK and abroad.
Composing: Many works for the concert hall, and recently a children's musical written with Adrian Mitchell *The Last Wild Wood in Sector 88*.

Royal Shakespeare Company

Sponsored by
Royal Insurance

Stratford-upon-Avon Box Office (0789) 295623

ROYAL SHAKESPEARE THEATRE

Julius Caesar
by William Shakespeare

The Merchant of Venice
by William Shakespeare

Twelfth Night
by William Shakespeare

The Taming of the Shrew
by William Shakespeare

Measure for Measure
by William Shakespeare

SWAN THEATRE

Hyde Park
by James Shirley

Titus Andronicus
by William Shakespeare

The Jew of Malta
by Christopher Marlowe

Sponsored by
Herald Press

The Revenger's Tragedy
by Cyril Tourneur

The New Inn
by Ben Jonson

THE OTHER PLACE

Fashion
by Doug Lucie
presented by arrangement with Michael Codron

Indigo
by Heidi Thomas

A Question of Geography
by John Berger and Nella Bielski

Cymbeline
by William Shakespeare

London Box Office (01) 638 8891

BARBICAN THEATRE

The Balcony
by Jean Genet

The Winter's Tale
by William Shakespeare

A Midsummer Night's Dream
by William Shakespeare

The Wizard of Oz
by L Frank Baum
*With music and lyrics by Harold Arlen and
E Y Harburg, adapted by John Kane.*

THE PIT

Deathwatch/The Maids
by Jean Genet

Old Year's Eve
by Peter Speyer

The Art of Success
by Nick Dear

Speculators
by Tony Marchant

MERMAID THEATRE

Box Office (01) 236 5568

Sarcophagus
by Vladimir Gubaryev

The Rover
by Aphra Behn

RSC in the West End

PALACE THEATRE

Box Office (01) 434 0909

Les Misérables
The Victor Hugo Musical

AMBASSADORS THEATRE

Box Office (01) 836 6111

Les Liaisons Dangereuses
by Christopher Hampton

THE OLD VIC

Box Office (01) 928 7616

Kiss Me Kate
Cole Porter's musical

Mermaid Theatre

Sponsored by
Royal Insurance

Royal Shakespeare Company

Incorporated under Royal Charter as the Royal Shakespeare Theatre
Patron Her Majesty The Queen
President Sir Kenneth Cork
Chairman of the Council Geoffrey A Cass
Vice-Chairman Dennis L Flower
Advisory Director Peggy Ashcroft, Peter Brook, Trevor Nunn
Artistic Director and Chief Executive Terry Hands
Direction Bill Alexander, John Barton, John Caird, Ron Daniels,
Terry Hands, Barry Kyle, Adrian Noble
Director Emeritus Trevor Nunn

Technical Services Administrator John Bradley
General Manager David Brierley
Publicity Controller Peter Harlock
Production Controller James Langley
Planning Controller Tim Leggatt
Senior Administrator Genista McIntosh
Barbican Administrator James Sargant
Financial Controller William Wilkinson

Artistic Director Mermaid Theatre Ron Daniels
Casting Siobhan Bracke
Publicity Stephen Browning
Press Caro Newling (01-628 3351)
Marketing Des Carr
Company Manager Trevor Williamson

For Eddie Kulukundis

Production Management P.M.A.
General Manager Jean Moore
Assistant to the General Manager Catherine Bone

For Gomba Holdings (UK) Ltd

General Manager Barbara Penney

Production credits for *The Rover*

Scenery made by RST workshops.
Costumes made by RST workshops. Additional costumes made by
Kate Wyatt, Wallace & McMurray, David Garret.
Wardrobe care by Robin Starch, tights by Elbeo.
Buns supplied by Peter Stratton.
Research by Leona Heimfeld. RSC programme compiled by Jo Denbury.

For the Mermaid Theatre

Technical Manager Forbes Nelson
Conference and Exhibition Manager Alison Heys
House Manager Christopher Playford
Box Office Manager Sarah Eastwood (01 236 5568)
Chief Electrician Lorraine Richards
Master Carpenter Patrick Ayling
Sound Operator Robin Nash
Wardrobe Supervisor Karen Marsh
Wardrobe Maintenance Louse De Ville Morel
Wigs and Make-up Julie Wright
Accounts Stuart Wise
Catering Manager Jacqueline Thomson

Food and Drink

Bridge Bar
A traditionally stocked bar (including draught beers) open for lunch
12-3pm, before and after performances from 5pm.
Dockyard Wine Bar
Open before show from 5pm – interesting wine line and wide selection of
bottled beers.
Food Bar
Open for lunch and pre-performance (times as above), serving home-made
soups, house specialities and fruit salad; and a wide range of salads and
gateaux. Patrons wishing to eat after the performance please place your
order before the show.

Commentary

compiled by Simon Trussler

Sources and Stage History

In a postscript to the first edition of *The Rover*, published in 1677, Aphra Behn thought it necessary to defend herself against charges of plagiarism: but she made no secret of her debt to Thomas Killigrew's earlier play *Thomaso; or, The Wanderer*, which had been written without any expectation of performance during the interregnum, in 1654, and published in Killigrew's *Comedies and Tragedies* ten years later. Mrs. Behn claims that she might as well be accused of taking her ideas from Richard Brome's *The Novella*, first performed in 1632: but whereas she borrowed from Brome only in minor matters of construction, and perhaps for a faint original of her Angellica, *The Rover* is clearly obliged to Killigrew's play in its general plot outline, and there are also some stylistic echoes. A comparison of her Willmore and Ned Blunt with Killigrew's counterparts, Thomaso and Edwardo, however, shows how far her skill in characterization transcends her source, just as she is superior to the prolix Killigrew in sustaining the dramatic pace, and in her tightness of construction.

Like so many of Mrs. Behn's plays, *The Rover* was first performed in the Dorset Garden Theatre, which had been planned for the Duke of York's company under Davenant, but was opened after his death with Thomas Betterton as joint manager in 1671. The first recorded performance of the play was on 24 March 1677, when Charles II was present to see Betterton take the role of Belvile, with his wife Mary as Florinda. Betterton's friend, the versatile actor William Smith, played Willmore, and the brilliant low comedian Cave Underhill took the part of Ned Blunt. Elizabeth Barry, who was to become better known for her tragic roles, played Hellena, and Anne Quin was Angellica.

Although the play was revived every few years until the turn of the century – at least in 1680, 1685, and 1696, sometimes at royal command – it was in the first half of the eighteenth century that it became firmly established in the repertoire, from which it was absent for only a single season between 1703 and 1743. Following in the footsteps of Will Mountfort's Willmore – 'dangerous to see', according to Queen Mary, because 'he made vice so alluring' – Robert Wilks often took the role early in the new century, although Verbruggen, Ryan, and Giffard were also seen in the part. Among the many Hellenas were Mrs. Verbruggen, Anne Oldfield, Mrs. Mountfort, Mrs. Rogers, Mrs. Bradshaw, Mrs. Bullock, Mrs. Bracegirdle, Mrs Vincent, and later Peg Woffington. Mrs. Barry had graduated to Angellica by 1707.

A revival at Covent Garden in 1757 – with Ned Shuter following in the footsteps of Estcourt, Penkethman, and Theophilus Cibber to make an outstanding Blunt – led to further productions in the following four seasons, but the play then disappeared from the repertoire until 1790, when an adaptation entitled *Love in Many Masks* was put together by Kemble for Drury Lane. The need for his tasteful but debilitating bowdlerisation sufficiently suggests why the stage history of *The Rover* was then interrupted for the best part of two hundred years.

Synopsis

'The rover' is the philandering cavalier Willmore, a naval adventurer who meets up with his fellow exiles from Cromwell's rule – the mercenary soldiers Belvile and Frederick, and the rustic gull Ned Blunt – in a Spanish colony, as the pre-Lenten carnival is about to begin. The eldest of three sisters, Florinda, is in love with Belvile, but is intended by her father to marry an elderly suitor, and by her brother Don Pedro for his own friend, the viceroy's son Don Antonio. The sprightly Hellena, reluctantly preparing to take the veil, and the demure but calculating Valeria plan with her to disguise themselves, join in the celebrations, and look out for men.

Antonio and Pedro fall out over the charms of the courtesan Angellica, who is demanding an outrageous thousand crowns for her favours; but she is eventually seduced into giving them gratis to the flamboyant but impoverished Willmore, of whom she becomes wildly jealous when she catches him later paying court to Hellena, in her gypsy disguise. Florinda has meanwhile arranged a midnight meeting with Belvile at her garden gate, but before his arrival she is accosted by the drunken Willmore, who disturbs the whole house.

As Belvile reproaches his friend, they observe Antonio about to enter Angellica's house, and Willmore wounds his rival – but it is Belvile who is arrested. Belvile is brought before Don Antonio, who resigns his own interest in Florinda to him in return for Belvile agreeing to stand in for Antonio in the duel planned with Don Pedro. Belvile almost gets possession of his mistress as a result, but is thwarted yet again by the untimely arrival of Willmore.

Hellena now fans the flames of jealousy between Angellica and Willmore, while Florinda, fleeing from her brother, finds herself in the hands of Ned Blunt – intent on avenging himself against women for the trick by which the prostitute Lucetta has deprived him of his possessions and his dignity. But his friends arrive in time to prevent a rape, Florinda's identity is discovered, and she and Belvile secure a priest to marry them, of whose services Valeria and Frederick also take advantage. Willmore is rescued by Antonio from death at the hands of the vengeful Angellica, but not from marriage at the hands of Hellena. Don Pedro reluctantly resigns himself to events.

Aphra Behn: a Brief Chronology

1640 *c.* Born, conjecturally in early July, at Wye or Sturry, near Canterbury, Kent. Maiden name Amies, Johnson, or Cooper.

1663 *c.* Family in Surinam, but her father, who had been appointed Lieutenant-General, died on the voyage. Stayed on a local plantation.

1664 Returned to London in the spring. Presented an Indian costume to the King's Company.

1665 *c.* Marriage to Mr. Behn, probably a Dutch merchant, who died soon afterwards, perhaps during the Great Plague.

1666 Persuaded by Thomas Killigrew to serve as a spy in the Dutch Wars, but discovered little of value while in Antwerp, and remained unpaid for her services. Great Fire of London in her absence.

1667 Returned to London.

1668 Committed to prison for debt, despite petitions to Killigrew and the King. Date of release uncertain.

1670 Beginning of her career as a professional writer. December, her first play, the tragi-comic *The Forced Marriage*, performed by the Duke's Company at Lincoln's Inn Fields, with Betterton in the lead, achieving a run of six nights. Around this time, beginning of her long relationship with the dissolute lawyer John Hoyle.

1671 Her second tragi-comedy, *The Amorous Prince*, at Lincoln's Inn Fields in the spring.

1672 Possibly edited the collection of poetry, *The Covent-Garden Drollery*.

1673 Feb., failure of her comedy of intrigue *The Dutch Lover* at Dorset Garden.

1676 The passionate tragedy *Abdelazer* performed at Dorset Garden in July, followed there in September by a 'scandalous' comedy with brothel scenes, *The Town Fop*.

1677 March, *The Rover* produced at Dorset Garden. Two other plays attributed to her also seen at Dorset Garden, *The Debauchee* in February and *The Counterfeit Bridegroom* in September.

1678 January, *Sir Patient Fancy*, a comedy adapted from Molière's *The Imaginary Invalid*, at Dorset Garden. The Popish Plot 'revealed' by Titus Oates.

1679 Beginning of the exclusion crisis. The comedy *The Feigned Courtesans* seen in the spring, and the tragi-comedy *The Young King* in early autumn, both at Dorset Garden.

1680 Death of John Wilmot, Earl of Rochester, aged 33.

1681 April, *The Second Part of The Rover*; November, the farcical comedy *The False Count*; and December, the historical comedy *The Roundheads:* all at Dorset Garden.

1682 The anti-Whig political lampoon *The City Heiress* 'well-received' at Dorset Garden in the spring, but *Like Father, Like Son* which failed there, remained unprinted, and is now lost apart from prologue and epilogue. Increasing hostility from the Whigs leads to her arrest for the 'abusive' and 'scandalous' prologue she contributed in August to the anonymous *Romulus and Hersilia*: she was probably let off with a caution. Merging of the two theatre companies.

1683 Wrote three of her posthumously-published short novels, and the first part of *Love Letters between a Nobleman and His Sister*.

1684 Published her *Poems on Several Occasions*.

1685 Publication of her poetic *Miscellany*. Death of Charles II and accession of his brother James II.

1686 The prose work *La Montre; or, The Lover's Watch* published. Returned to the theatre in April with the comedy *The Lucky Chance* at Drury Lane.

1687 The *commedia*-style farce *The Emperor of the Moon*, one of her greatest successes, first seen at Drury Lane in March. Arrest and inconclusive trial of John Hoyle for sodomy.

1688 Published the short novels *The Fair Jilt, Agnes de Castro*, and *Oroonoko*, the latter based on her experiences in Surinam. The 'bloodless revolution' leads to the abdication of James II, and the protestant supremacy under William and Mary.

1689 16 April, died, and buried in Westminster Abbey. Posthumous production in November of her last play, the comedy *The Widow Ranter* at Drury Lane, a failure. The comedy *The Younger Brother* also first produced posthumously, at Drury Lane in February 1696.

'The wit of her comedies seems to be generally acknowledged, and it is equally acknowledged that they are very indecent, on which account I have not thought myself under any obligation to peruse them. It would have been an unworthy employment, nicely to estimate a wit which, having been applied to the purposes of impiety and vice, ought not only to be held in the utmost detestation, but consigned, if possible, to eternal oblivion.'

Dr. Kippis (1778)

The Return of the Banished Cavaliers

The events which restored Charles II to the English throne in May 1660 were fast-moving: as late as September 1659, both Charles and his brother James had appeared to be making plans for an indefinite exile. Much had to be done during the new king's 'honeymoon' with his people, and it is a measure of the importance attached by Charles to theatrical matters that he seems to have given no less urgent attention to sorting out the squabbles between the various entrepreneurs vying to form new theatrical companies than to reconciling the old enemies of the civil war.

Exile for Charles had been, after his apparently final defeat at Worcester in 1651, a relatively comfortable affair, passed mainly in the civilised if often conspiratorial surroundings of Paris and Brussels: but for many of the followers of the king and his 'martyred' father, the interregnum was spent in a constant struggle against hardship. Some laid low at home, their estates confiscated or sold off piecemeal to meet fines for their 'delinquency'. Others, like Belvile and Willmore in *The Rover*, turned soldiers or sailors of fortune, accumulating mistresses, booty, or battle honours with an equally casual loyalty.

Most of the young Restoration gallants, now returning along with their king, would thus in all probability have spent a childhood or adolescence in the turbulent atmosphere of civil war, the early years of their adult life cut off from family traditions and that sense of service which possession of land could still, on occasion, encourage. Nor did the Restoration settlement return the estates sold off by persecuted royalists to 'upstart' puritan landgrabbers. Lacking roots, but often bearing a load of such grudges, these 'rovers' saw little reason not to pursue in England the kind of desperate sexual and economic opportunism which had become habitual – and was now also reflected in the theatre to which they flocked.

Besides, there was even a sort of theological justification for living out the belief that 'debauchery was loyalty, gravity rebellion'. Anything that inverted the detested values of puritanism had its own validity – and, as it happened, an open delight in sexual dalliance (as in theatricality) happened to coincide with the tastes of the restored monarch. No wonder that Charles's court in Whitehall proved such a magnet, and that its values so permeated the life and attitudes of 'the town' – which, it should be remembered, meant the fashionable residential and shopping area of which Covent Garden was the heart and the Strand the main artery, as distinct from 'the city', whose tradesmen and financiers, tainted with puritan sympathies, became the 'cits' so often mocked in the prologues, epilogues, and cuck-oldings of Restoration comedy.

That the king no less than his courtiers were often dependent on the financial assistance of such people made it, of course, all the more necessary to display them as semi-illiterate upstarts in the theatre – which they nevertheless also attended, sometimes in such numbers as to spoil Samuel Pepys's enjoyment. The tensions of a nation and a capital which remained so divided were reflected in the microcosmic conditions of its theatre: and although the ostensible world of *The Rover* is that of exile in a faraway country, its values are those of men restored to their country, but not to their own.

The thwarting of an aged father's wish to marry his daughter to a rich but geriatric suitor is an age-old theme of comedy: but whereas the contemporary *commedia* made prominent characters of its Pantaloons and their doddering friends, it is significant that Mrs. Behn keeps Florinda's stern father and the farting Don Vincentio permanently off-stage. The traditional struggles between the values of youth and age, poverty and wealth, give way here to just the kind of internecine, sexual warfare through which the 'banished cavaliers' of real life continued to forget – or to sublimate – their sorrows.

'From Aphra Behn's point of view *The Rover* was her most outright and positive celebration of those cavalier childhood heroes. Here with the 'masculine' part of her, her poetry as she was to describe it in the preface to *The Lucky Chance*, she could be one of them at last. But as the writer is rarely just one person among a fictitious crowd so I believe, though her identification with the cavaliers is intense, that she was at the same time AB, the courtesan Angellica Bianca. Her trade was words, and it was impossible that she shouldn't have noticed those initials. Perhaps that was why she chose [Killigrew's] play.'

Maureen Duffy (1977)

'For Aphra Behn, writing was an act of sexual politics, a balancing of the powers of "masculine" intellect and "feminine" charm (as intellect and charm were conceived of as gendered subjects in the seventeenth century) in a daring leap toward freedom of speech and action for women. She was principally concerned with what might be called the public and private faces of women's oppression in the society of seventeenth-century England. Contemporary marriage customs which forced women into marriage for lack of any other recourse represented the public face of the oppression; the private face was the unspoken distrust of and prejudice against women writers.'

Cheri Davis Langdell (1985)

The King, the Court, and the Courtesans

The character of Charles II might very easily have been conceived as the hero of a Wycherley play – dour, cynical, and introverted at heart, yet capable of a pretty wit, and sexually attractive beyond the advantages of *force majeure*. Whether his personality was shaped by exile, or simply well-adapted to it, the fact remains that, before the Restoration, Charles enjoyed the semblance of both power and responsibility without the reality of either: life became, in short, a form of playacting. Later, when the king strolled, supposedly incognito but recognised by all, into the House of Lords to listen to a debate, he would duly declare the entertainment as good as a play, and sardonically join in the laughter at veiled references to himself.

In exile, Charles had pursued his women with no less fervour than Willmore or Belvile in *The Rover*. The shadow cast over his marriagability by the attempts of one of his early mistresses, Lucy Walter, to declare herself his lawful wife ironically allowed him all the more freedom to engage in other affairs, for which he sought among his own camp-followers, the nobility of the French court, and the brothels of Paris with a fine impartiality which led one of his recent biographers, J.P. Kenyon, to describe him as 'not a gourmet so much as a gourmand' in sexual matters.

Back home, Charles's male companions were drawn largely from a promiscuous, hard-drinking, but highly-literate set which included, besides the notorious Earl of Rochester, the Duke of Buckingham, Sir George Etherege, and Charles Sedley – all playwrights, as much probably from fashion as inspiration, just as in other ages courtiers might have been concerned to excel at hunting deer, jousting, or grouse-shooting. These were men to whom casual violence came readily, and who walked that uneasy tightrope between rape and seduction, or between brutality and the defence of honour, which is so often reflected in the plays they wrote and watched. A regular attender at the theatres, Charles himself is said to have lent a hand in the writing of plays, and he also interested himself in matters of casting. He both encouraged and emulated the Restoration 'style', in dramatic art as in life – and apparently displayed it as freely among women of good breeding as among his male cronies or his concubines. It made for sexual equality, of a sort.

When the dynastic imperative finally cornered the king into marriage, he took to wife the unfortunate princess Catherine of Braganza – in part to safeguard the alliance with her native Portugal, in part to produce for him an unquestionably legitimate heir. This, perhaps by way of unconscious vengeance, she resolutely failed to do – so perpetuating the long drawn-out crisis over the ever-likelier succession of Charles's Catholic brother, James. The king's treatment of his wife in many ways epitomised the double standards of Restoration comedy. In private, he humiliated her by appointing his own mistresses – successively, Barbara Villiers, Countess of Castlemaine, and Louise de Kéroualle, Duchess of Portsmouth – as ladies of her bedchamber. Yet in public his curious sense of honour combined with his political instinct, and when the Whigs backed Titus Oates's allegations of Catherine's complicity in a plot to poison her husband, they misjudged their man. Charles refused to put away his wife, the allegations collapsed – and the Whigs, by then espousing the cause of Charles's illegitimate son, Monmouth, lost all credibility, along with their hopes of excluding James from the succession.

Mrs. Behn flayed the Whigs with impunity in *The City Heiress* in 1682, but when she extended her target to include Monmouth himself, in the sniping prologue she contributed to *Romulus and Hersilia* later that year, she was arrested, and at least severely reprimanded. Charles's affection for his unruly bastard son, or some perverse sense of his far-flung family's dignity, never entirely deserted him – nor, of course, did he forget his mistresses, of whom two of the most prominent came from the theatre. Mary Davis he took from the Duke's company, and the almost legendary Nell Gwyn from the King's – where her position was due to real talent and wit as well as to her undoubted beauty. When her coach was mistaken for the Catholic Duchess of Portsmouth's at the height of the exclusion crisis, Nell entirely won over a jostling mob by declaring from the window, 'Pray, good people, be civil. I am the *protestant* whore!' The line displays all the wry, self-aware sexuality of one of Aphra Behn's new women. The two were, in fact, close friends.

Even in death, Charles exhibited something like the last-act repentance of a rake from Restoration comedy: at the prompting of Lady Portsmouth, he was attended by a priest, and made a deathbed conversion to Catholicism – the priest, by a fine irony, taking the covert, backstairs route to his bedchamber well-worn by so many of Charles's mistresses. And among his last words were those of commendation to his brother James: 'Let not poor Nelly starve.' In a room filled with as many illegitimate offspring as could be hastily assembled, neither Nell Gwyn nor any of his other women were permitted to pay their last respects. Poor Nelly, as it happened, died of an apoplexy soon after, but the Duchess of Mazarin lived on, through reaction and revolution, to die still in receipt of a royal pension in 1699. There is little in Restoration comedy which exceeds Charles's personal excesses, or typifies better than his own conduct the mixture of calculation and generosity – and the downright double-standards – which characterised the Restoration 'wit'.

The Altered Face of the Stage

'They altered at once the whole face of the stage by introducing scenes and women' – or so John Dennis claimed nostalgically, writing in 1725 of the events of 1660, when play-acting was once more permitted after being banned by the puritans since 1642. The court masques of the Jacobean and Caroline theatre had, it's true, employed quite elaborate scenery, and the open-air theatres of the Elizabethans had long been giving way to indoor 'private' theatres, with greater potential for technical effects. The difference now was that the proscenium arch formed a 'picture-frame' for the painted perspective scenery, changed by the wings-and-shutters system, which provided a formalised background to Restoration comedy and tragedy.

But it was *only* a background: the actors performed on the extensive apron stage in front of the proscenium, in a relationship with their audiences no less intimate and uncluttered than their forebears. Indeed, Restoration theatres, which seated from around five to eight hundred, were actually smaller than the Elizabethan public playhouses, and their audiences, although not drawn quite so exclusively from a courtly elite as has sometimes been suggested, certainly felt themselves to be part of a social as much as a theatrical occasion.

Quite how that 'crossing of the boundary' between actor and character, so clearly felt in Restoration prologues and epilogues, affected the acting of the play itself is not certain: but the style would certainly have been presentational rather than realistic – at a time, confessedly, when rituals of 'presentation' were of great importance to everyday behaviour as well. So, with directors unthought of, and playwrights far less involved in the practical business of mounting a play than their Elizabethan counterparts, the influence of the dancing-master was probably strong in matters of movement and stage grouping. As Jocelyn Powell has aptly summed it up: 'The atmosphere of the Restoration theatre was that of a sophisticated cabaret.'

Of those bidding for the right to build their own companies amidst the political confusion of Charles's return, the successful 'patentees' were both men of influence at court, who had had experience of theatre before the civil wars. It was Thomas Killigrew who wrote the play on which Mrs. Behn based *The Rover* – but whereas his *Thomaso* had been intended for reading only, Sir William Davenant had even succeeded in getting plays with music produced under Cromwell's guard (so that English opera, as later with melodrama, began as a means of getting round the law). Davenant was given his royal patent to manage, under the patronage of the Duke of York, a company which first played in a converted 'real' tennis court at Lincoln's Inn Fields, and which moved in 1671 to Wren's Dorset Garden Theatre beside the Thames, where so many of Mrs. Behn's plays were performed. Killigrew's company, which came under the king's own patronage, played in another converted tennis court until the first Drury Lane Theatre was completed in 1663, to be replaced by a new playhouse in 1674 after its destruction by fire.

With just two companies of less than thirty players apiece – reduced to the single 'united' company from 1682 to 1695 – acting was thus an exclusive though not prestigious profession, its members as well-known personally to many in the audience as their own acquaintances in the pit or boxes. And, although the patents stressed that the introduction of actresses was a matter of morality – to correct the abuse of men appearing 'in the habits of women' – intimacy between these players and their audiences was not confined to closeness in the auditorium. It was probably inevitable that, in the absence of a traditional route for women into the profession, some actresses in a licentious age should have achieved their positions through sexual patronage – though it's also indisputable that Elizabeth Barry, despite her path being smoothed by the notorious rake Lord Rochester, became a truly great tragic actress, while Nell Gwyn, although she owed her early chances to being the mistress of a leading player, Charles Hart, became no less striking a comic actress before she caught the eye of the king.

Other actresses, such as the great Thomas Betterton's wife Mary, were nonetheless able to lead lives of untained virtue at a time when such behaviour in courtly society was almost eccentric – while the fine comic actress Anne Bracegirdle even managed to sustain a reputation for excessive prudishness in private life. This did not, however, prevent her being thought fair game for predatory males: as late as 1692, an assault on her honour was compounded by the murder of the actor William Mountford, who had tried to intervene on her behalf. Those guilty were not severely punished.

This was an age when Rochester might order Dryden to be beaten up in a back alley for an imagined satirical slight; when the king himself could instigate an assault upon a parliamentarian who had dared to criticise his mistresses; and when Rochester and Sedley could attempt the rape of an heiress in broad daylight. The mixture of violence and casual sexuality which Aphra Behn presents even less discreetly than most of her contemporaries is thus a reflection on the stage of the very brittle veneer of politeness which barely concealed the viciousness of much high-society life.

The Professionalism of Aphra Behn

Aphra Behn was not the first woman playwright: that distinction goes, curiously, to a tenth-century Benedictine nun named Hrotsvitha, who wrote six religious dramas while in the German abbey of Gandersheim. That Hrotsvitha's plays should glorify the virtue of chastity was only to be expected in a period when the typology of women allowed few gradations between the virgin and the whore, other than that of the nagging shrew – but it makes a wry contrast to the approach of her Restoration successors in the craft.

Mrs. Behn was not quite the earliest of these. The Marchioness of Newcastle published two collections, including some twenty plays, in 1662 and 1668, but these were purely 'closet dramas', and never performed. Catherine Phillips, however, achieved the honour of having her *Pompey*, a version of Corneille's play, performed in the brand new Smock Alley Theatre in Dublin in February 1663 – and so of inaugurating the vogue for 'heroic dramas', in the rhymed couplets which were to displace blank verse as the main medium for tragic writing until Buckingham's *The Rehearsal* helped to burlesque heroics off the stage in 1671.

Just as Catherine Phillips adopted the pen-name of Orinda, so Aphra Behn also allowed herself to be known as Astraea. But Mrs. Phillips had written purely for her own amusement, at a time when most male playwrights were courtiers and men of letters, often unconcerned with the income their plays produced – whereas Aphra Behn wrote from pressing financial need. The theatre of the period differed from Shakespeare's in that most playwrights were not formally attached to a particular company. Dryden's contract to write three plays a year in return for becoming a 'sharer' in the King's company was unusual – and unfulfilled. Generally, the professional writer was dependent upon the benefit system, whereby the profits of the third night's performance – and perhaps of the sixth, and very exceptionally of the ninth – were allocated to him. A good benefit could reap as much as £100, with a further lump sum possible for publication: but there was no guarantee that any play would even reach the third night, and it was thus as important that a sympathetic audience should give a good reception on the first night, as that a rich one (perhaps willing to make presents over the odds) should fill the house on the third.

Those males scandalised by Mrs. Behn, who dared to affront 'the modesty of her sex' by writing as bawdily as they, did not even deign to consider the element of economic necessity that drove her to satisfy the prevailing tastes of the town. She was among the more prolific of Restoration playwrights in part because she *had* to be – and the total of at least sixteen plays performed during her lifetime is thus in marked contrast with, say, Wycherley's four, or Congreve's six. When she declared in the preface to her late comedy *The Lucky Chance* (1686) that she was 'not content to write for a third night only', she may simply have been staking a claim to be writing for posterity as well as for money: but her invariable association with Dorset Garden from 1673 until the merging of the companies in 1682 may suggest some more formal arrangement with the Duke's company than the chances of the benefit system allowed.

The merger of the companies was a consequence of the decline in theatre attendances in the wake of the political crises of Charles's later years; and the United Company cut its costs still further by including a higher proportion of revivals, whose dead authors made no claim upon diminishing receipts. Other playwrights, such as Aphra's friends Thomas Otway and William Wycherley, fared no better, and John Dryden was forced to seek meagre government patronage. Classically-educated males could at least turn to publishing translations as an alternative source of income – whereas Mrs. Behn, in contributing to a version of Ovid, had to work from a literal first draft. Greek and Latin were no part of expected female 'accomplishments'.

Aphra Behn enjoyed renewed stage success in later life – notably with *The Lucky Chance* and the strikingly original *The Emperor of the Moon*. But increasingly – and in not dissimilar circumstances to her eighteenth-century successor, Henry Fielding – she turned from plays to writing novels. In 1688, the year before her death, she published *Oroonoko*, the work by which she probably remains best known – its anti-slavery theme anticipating Harriet Beecher Stowe, and its element of noble savagery even upstaging Rousseau. Whether or not she was the first 'true' novelist, before such aspirants as Defoe, Richardson, and Fielding himself, depends on one's definition of the form – a form in which, however, later women writers were to challenge masculine 'supremacy' with far greater success than, Aphra Behn excepted, they ever challenged male chauvinism in the theatre.

'With Mrs. Behn . . . we come to town and rub shoulders with ordinary people in the streets. Mrs. Behn was a middle-class woman with all the plebeian virtues of humour, vitality, and courage; a woman forced by the death of her husband and some unfortunate adventures of her own to make her living by her wits. She made, by working very hard, enough to live on. The importance of that fact outweighs anything she actually wrote. . . . For now that Aphra Behn had done it, girls could go to their parents and say, You need not give me an allowance; I can make money by my pen. Of course the answer for many years to come was, Yes, by living the life of Aphra Behn! Death would be better! and the door was slammed faster than ever.'

Virginia Woolf (1929)

The Sexual Economics of the Restoration

Charles Dickens may not actually have invented 'the values of family life' along with the traditional English Christmas, but it's undeniable that in much pre-romantic drama and literature there's little love lost between fathers and sons, elder and younger brothers, or husbands and wives. The death of a wealthy father or elder brother is more usually a matter for congratulation among the friends of the fortunate heir – while marriage, of course, has everything to do with the businesslike arrangement of property and dynasties, and very little to do with the affections.

True love, before marriage or after, is reserved for a mistress – though in most romantic comedies, where love is actually permitted to lead towards marriage, the hopeful suitor is usually assured, by luck or judgement, of a respectable fortune besides. In real life, the young couple might not even have met before their parents or go-betweens had finished arranging the match. (Ordinary working folk could, ironically, better 'afford' to marry for love the less they could afford anything else: but, until quite recently, ordinary working folk have not much figured in great literature or theatre, other than as comic relief.)

The matter was further complicated by the 'sexual revolution' which led Charles I to declare in 1664 that 'the passion of love is very much out of fashion in this country'. Even the once-adored mistress was now regarded as for sexual satisfaction only – an object of that curious combination of arousal and disgust which permeates the poems of such burnt-out rakes as Rochester. And the disgust is perhaps most readily heaped on those women who tried reciprocally to exercise the sexual freedom they had supposedly been granted.

In herself advocating a more liberal sexuality for women, Aphra Behn acknowledged, too, that the lack of an equivalent economic independence, combined with the fear or actuality of childbirth and the earlier loss of physical charms, constrained women from exercising their 'freedom' from a position of any other equality than that of their wits. And freedom of sexual movement was not freedom of *social* movement: the over-compliant mistress was still widely regarded as no better than a whore – to which status abandonment or decline could all too often reduce her. Mrs. Behn herself enjoyed the relative independence from male domination that only widowhood could bring – but not the inherited fortune that would have added security to freedom. If Restoration actresses also called themselves 'Mrs.' it was not because they had all been married, but because 'Miss' had come to be suggestive merely of sexual availability.

Aphra Behn was not above evading the problem in her plays – or rather, not above reconciling it as many writers had done and would do again, by such a device as she used in *The Dutch Lover*, where, for all her heroine's vaunted rebellion against paternal choice, her self-selected lover turns out to be her father's preferred suitor as well. And if the very title of her first play, *The Forced Marriage*, anticipates the importance of the theme to her writing, by her second, *The Amorous Prince*, she was falling back on the convention that the most promiscuous rake allows himself to be reformed in time for the final curtain.

The Town Fop showed the horrific consequences of a forced marriage, from which the participants are only released thanks to the hero's earlier, legally-binding pledge of marriage to his mistress. The father, meanwhile, has had time to see the awful consequences of his preferred alliance – which include the hero spending half his unwanted wife's portion on a wild debauch. But no resolution is offered by Mrs. Behn to the economic and sexual plight of that rejected wife – a 'loose end' not dissimilar to that in *The Rover* of the scorned Angellica, in whom the playwright seems to have invested a considerable, perhaps all too personal passion.

Aphra Behn, then, made no pretence of having resolved, dramatically or personally, all the problems posed by the combination of new attitudes to sexuality with very old attitudes to other kinds of freedom. In many ways she was no less equivocal or downright muddled about sex than most of her male counterparts – though she probably did recognise, along with her recent biographer Angeline Goreau, that the 'liberated' wits of the Restoration were fearfully if unconsciously obsessed with 'the possibility that women might have sexual desires that were independent of their role as passive receptacles of male desire'.

That Hellena in *The Rover* falls in love with Willmore for all the wrong reasons may tell us more about Aphra Behn's own unfortunate liaisons than about Hellena: but neither the character nor her creator was a 'passive receptacle'. What Behn did achieve, in her writing if not perhaps in her life, was a triumphant assertion of women's rights to their own sexuality, and at least the tentative expression – if her plays were to remain commercial, it could be no more than tentative – of her belief that true sexual satisfaction for both men *and* women lay in close and reciprocal relationships, not in the yoking of sexuality to property rights and family trees.

'Her very writing and her attitude toward it are acts of sexual politics. As practised by Behn's women characters and by Behn and other women playwrights of the Restoration . . . sexual politics was woman's resourceful exertion of whatever power she may have – sexual, social, economic, or political – so as to redress the social and psychosexual balance ever so slightly in her favour. If in Kate Millett's conception of sexual politics the term implies male domination of women in their sexual roles, in feminist and female writers of the Restoration sexual politics is the use of power by woman to achieve whatever she wants and *freely* chooses.'

Cheri Davis Langdell (1985)

'The Injuries of Age and Time'

For a woman whose plays make what appear to us quite proper claims for the independence of her sex, Aphra Behn numbered among her closest acquaintances many men – apart from the king himself, the likes of Sedley, Buckingham, and Rochester – who were liberated in their own sexuality, but unenlightened in their attitudes towards women. Rochester, like most of these courtly wits, was no 'mere' rake; and is even credited with training one of his mistresses, Elizabeth Barry, for the stage: characteristically, however, he undertook the exercise not so much from interest in her own non-sexual attributes, but for a wager with his male companions. Aphra Behn was not only indebted to Rochester as a patron, but also appears genuinely to have liked and admired the man, with whom she exchanged bawdy poems. A chronic drunkard as well as a poet, a ravisher of pretty women and a fancier of young boys, Rochester, who was generally considered the model for the fashionable wit Dorimant in Etherege's *The Man of Mode*, was capable of scandalising even the king's sense of decency with some of his more public outrages.

Rochester may well have been on Mrs. Behn's mind when she tried to make Willmore in *The Rover* so sexually magnetic. But there were others in Aphra's circle with a claim to be the model for such a character. There was John Greenhill, the highly talented portrait painter, who, like Rochester, died of his excesses in his early thirties. Aphra Behn wrote an elegy to his memory and sent a copy to Rochester: he had at least been spared 'the injuries of age and time'. In lighter-hearted vein, she made poetic mock of another male acquaintance for his misfortune in contracting syphilis – not an uncommon ailment in her circle, and one from which Mrs. Behn was possibly herself a sufferer in later years. If so, she probably picked up the disease during the longest and stormiest of her own love affairs, with the bisexual rake, lawyer, man of letters, and chief claimant to be the original of Willmore – John Hoyle.

Suspected of the republican sympathies which had led his father to take his own life, Hoyle was in other respects entirely a man of the Restoration. He was attractive to women, and appears to have treated all his conquests with the amused contempt which so exasperated Aphra Behn. Her poems suggest that, despite her own previous liaisons, this affair – which would have been at its tempestuous height around the time she was writing *The Rover* – was the one in which she felt the most complete consummation of her sexual passion. Yet Hoyle kept Aphra, like all his mistresses, at a distance, pursuing his other affairs while wishing Aphra to remain faithful to him alone; inflicting casual insults upon her, yet highly sensitive to any imagined slights in her own behaviour.

Aphra Behn's remaining letters to Hoyle seem to be half-persuading, half-pleading for the kind of freedom, combined with commitment of the heart, to which Hellena in *The Rover* believes she

had led Willmore. But Aphra's biographer Angeline Goreau suggests that part of Hoyle's attraction was precisely the knowledge that she would never be called upon to act out the role of wife for him, any more than that of conventional mistress. She suffered, but she kept her freedom. So, presumably, did her Hellena – who failed conspicuously to appear alongside the merry widower Willmore in *The Second Part of The Rover*.

The death of Charles II in 1685 marked the close of an era that had already turned sour. John Hoyle was tried inconclusively for sodomy in 1687, by which time the affair with Aphra was probably over. He outlived her only by three years, before being killed in a tavern brawl – for which his murderer successfully pleaded self defence. Greenhill and Rochester were already dead, burned out by debauchery, and Buckingham was not only out of favour politically but 'worn to a thread with whoring'. Among Aphra Behn's play writing friends, Wycherley was in a debtors' prison, Nathaniel Lee was on public exhibition in a madhouse, and Otway was starving to death in a slum – despite, it seems, some financial help from Aphra, although she was personally in debt. She herself died with a fine sense of timing, a few days after the coronation of William and Mary, whose accession ended the Stuart dynasty with whose values Mrs. Behn was so closely identified. *The Rover*, written in 1677, just a year before the 'Popish Plot', may in retrospect be seen as one of the last celebrations of the Restoration spirit, in which no sense of doubt or danger lurks in the darker corners of bedchamber or tavern.

'In the preface to her third play, *The Dutch Lover*, [Aphra Behn] explicitly disclaimed the existence of theme or moral in her writings; nevertheless, broken or loveless marriages and the distress caused by arranged marriages appear in a majority of her works. Like Otway, she was concerned with tracing the effects of broken friendship. . . .'

A.H. Scouten (1976)

'[The Willmore of *The Second Part of The Rover*] is even more Wilmot than in Part One. Hellena, whom he married at the end of the first part, had died, and he is now in Madrid and in pursuit of a famous courtesan, La Nuche, played by Elizabeth Barry. This too couldn't have escaped many in the audience. Rochester's affair with Elizabeth Barry was well known. Here she was in effect playing herself. Appropriately in the end she agrees to go away with Willmore without the benefit of marriage, which he describes as "formal foppery".'

Maureen Duffy (1977)

The Rover' as Restoration Comedy

The critic of Aphra Behn's plays finds himself (or, more often of late, herself) in a paradoxical position. The works are inseparably linked with those social and political conditions which I have tried to outline in earlier sections, as they are to their author's personal feelings about those conditions. Yet we know so few details of Aphra's life, outside her purely professional activities, that any conjectural reconstruction inevitably leads us . . . back full-circle to the plays themselves.

Perhaps the chief gain from getting caught up in this critical double-bind is the way in which characters in her plays – which one would otherwise tend to categorise as 'types' – come to take on ampler dimensions. There was an influential book of my student years called *The Gay Couple in Restoration Comedy* – which might valuably have explored the homosexual elements its title now seems to suggest, but which in those days was concerned with witty gallants and their pert mistresses. It would thus have 'placed' Willmore and Hellena in a convenient literary lineage which stretched from Beatrice and Benedick to Mirabell and Millamant . . . and extended, for that matter, to Jack Tanner and Ann Whitefield. It suggested, in short, a tradition which has more to do with the 'enduring' psychological interest of love-hate relationships, or the downright metaphysical workings of some Shavian life-force, than with the societies in which such forms of sexual masquerade could be enacted. But Mrs. Behn's 'gay couple' in *The Rover* conduct their duels of wit within a complex web of sexual, social, and economic prejudices inseparable from their time.

Or, to take a different tangent: the character regarded by most critics, even the most sympathetic, as an unsatisfactory loose-end to the plot, Angellica Bianca, becomes, through her acronymic as well as her temperamental similarity to her creator . . . not anything as simple as an authorial mouthpiece, or as theatrically irrelevant as a self-portrait, but a 'loose-end' left over by society itself. Angellica is the sexually-attractive woman who has rejected the loss of independence involved in marriage: she has therefore exploited her only form of inherited 'capital' – her looks – in part as revenge against the male sex, which has reduced her to that expedient. But the repudiation by Willmore represents for her not just the scorning of real love painfully exposed, but a first reminder that loss of beauty will leave her with a future of economic uncertainty as well as personal loneliness.

When L. C. Knights launched his influential attack on Restoration comedy just before the Second World War, he was using the term in its commonly vague sense, to embrace the work of Congreve, Vanbrugh, and even Farquhar – all of whom wrote long after the values of the 'chronological' Restoration had been extinguished, and who were all too conscious of the moral critique of their work initiated in 1698 by Jeremy Collier. A century or so later,

all that an apologetic Charles Lamb could suggest by way of excuse for these dissolute comedies was that they were 'artificial', set in a 'Utopia of gallantry' with 'no reference whatsoever to the world that is'. Whether or not that is true of the later plays of Congreve and Vanbrugh, Aphra Behn helps us to view the actual world of the Restoration from a new angle which also gives appropriate depth to the work of Etherege, Otway, or Wycherley, and confirms that all are writing about a very 'real' if limited range of experience.

The Rover, of course, is unusual in that it is not set in the fashionable West End drawing-rooms and walks of Restoration London, but in a recent past to which a due proportion of its audiences in 1677 probably looked back a mite nostalgically. True, this is still the world of 'the town', and the foolish country gull Ned Blunt can expect to fall into its snares as surely as he would have done in London: but the advantage of 'foreignness' also means that Belvile and his companions are less sure-footed socially, just as they are free of the constraints of class expectations or family ties. And such, as I have suggested earlier, are probably among the underlying causes of the 'actual' Restoration spirit.

And so, perhaps a trifle schematically, Aphra Behn shows her exiles spanning a whole spectrum of attitudes to women and to love – from the mere loutishness of Blunt, through the butterfly charm of Willmore, to the romantic single-heartedness of Belvile. Each has his theatrical ancestors, but each is also part of an historical moment. Each meets his match, and gets his sexual if not his moral desserts.

All moral judgements are relative. When Gilbert Burnet cautioned Rochester against womanising, his ostensibly Christian grounds of reproof were that it was wrong to rob a father or a husband of their property. When Hellena casts off her gypsy disguise and reveals that she has a fortune at her disposal, the *only* choice she has in deciding its and her own fate is between a nunnery and marriage. In declaring for Willmore, she is 'disposing' of her fortune indeed. It *should* not have been so, of course: but precisely because Mrs. Behn's characters are *not* living in Charles Lamb's artificial world, it would have been pointless for her to attempt any more 'morally appropriate' conclusion. The only alternative is the semi-independence enjoyed by Angellica, and Mrs. Behn does not attempt to suggest a conclusion to that.

Many of those parents who preferred to trust their own financial acumen rather than their daughter's emotional inclinations in choosing her a husband sincerely believed that lasting security was more important to a woman than fleeting sexual excitement. Restoration comedy occasionally twisted the rules of the game by allowing the two to coincide – but it also accepted that 'rules' which did not generally relate love to marriage therefore permitted love outside marriage. The alleged hypocrisy of such plays is arguably the reverse – an openness, confessedly uncritical, about a state of sexual affairs which continued well into the Victorian era, although by that time such openness was found offensive.

Our own century's response to Restoration comedy suggests that it continues to touch us near the quick. It was only permissible as a kind of make-believe once the romantics had idealised sexual relationships without altering their economic base; but it came into a somewhat prettified version of its own during the nineteen-twenties, when a fresh wave of the sexual revolution broke – but again touched only the upper classes. Once the bright young things were swept away, it suffered stern critical rebuffs in the self-improving 'forties, until the 'permissive society' seemed to be spreading a gospel of sexual openness to all sections of society. Then came the feminist consciousness that 'openness' no more meant equality in the nineteen-seventies than it had in the sixteen-seventies.

As a feminist in her own time, that is one of the things that Mrs. Behn had been saying all along. As a professional playwright with no alternative source of income, she could not, however, say it very loudly. That was *her* critical double-bind.

For Further Reading

There is no adequate modern edition of Mrs. Behn's complete works. The fullest, but textually unsatisfactory collection is *The Works*, edited in six volumes by Montague Summers (London, 1915), subsequently available in a facsimile reprint (New York: Phaeton Press, 1967). Both parts of *The Rover* are in the first volume. There is a useful but now out-of-print edition of our play edited by Frederick M. Link in the Regents Restoration Drama Series (London: Arnold, 1967), and it was also included in the second volume of *Restoration Comedy*, edited by A.N. Jeffares (London, 1974). Of Aphra Behn's other plays, *The Dutch Lover* is included in a useful one-volume selection of her works, *Selected Writings of the Ingenious Mrs. Aphra Behn*, edited by Robert Phelps (New York: Grove Press, 1950). *The Emperor of the Moon* is in *Ten English Farces*, edited by Leo Hughes and A.H. Scouten (Austin: University of Texas Press, 1948), while *The Lucky Chance* is available both in a separate edition (London: Methuen, 1984) and in an anthology, *The Female Wits*, edited by Fidelis Morgan (London: Virago, 1981), which, besides helpful background material, also assembles work by four of Behn's near-contemporaries – plus the male-chauvinist lampoon against them from which the anthology takes its title. Mrs. Behn's best-known novel, *Oroonoko*, is readily accessible in an Everyman collection *Shorter Novels: Jacobean and Restoration*, edited by Philip Henderson (London: Dent, 1930), and will be published in a single edition by Methuen in October 1986.

Among the biographies of Behn, the earliest modern work, V. Sackville-West's brief *Aphra Behn: the Incomparable Astrea* (London: Gerald Howe, 1927) is now more revealing of its author than its subject. George Woodcock's *The Incomparable Aphra* (London: Boardman, 1948) remains of interest, but Emily Hahn's *Aphra Behn* (London: Cape, 1951) is less substantial than its length might suggest. W.J. Cameron's *New Light on Aphra Behn* (University of Auckland Press, 1961) was important for scholars in restoring limited authority to the anonymous and long-disputed *Life and Memoirs* of 1696, but its findings have been incorporated and supplemented in two more recent biographies, Maureen Duffy's *The Passionate Shepherdess: Aphra Behn* (London: Cape, 1977) and Angeline Goreau's *Reconstructing Aphra* (Oxford University Press, 1980). This latter illuminatingly recreates the socio-political context in which Aphra wrote, while the former is more pertinently critical about the works themselves. Frederick M. Link's *Behn* (New York: Twayne, 1968) is the only full-length critical study, but all three of these last titles include extensive bibliographies.

Despite the recent upsurge of interest in feminist writing there is suprisingly little, apart from Fidelis Morgan's collection cited above, offering adequate coverage of this aspect of the Restoration period. Exceptions are Rosamond Gilder's *Enter the Actress* (London: Harrap, 1931), a pioneering study far wider in scope than its title suggests; and Nancy Cotton's *Women Playwrights in England, c. 1363-1750* (Lewisburg: Bucknell University Press, 1980). Henry W. Lanier's *The First English Actresses* (New York, 1931), E.J. Gagen's *The New Woman: Her Emergence in English Drama* (New York, 1954), and J.H. Wilson's *All the King's Ladies* (Chicago, 1958) remain of interest, while this last author's *The Court Wits of the Restoration* (Princeton, 1948) provides a broader socio-literary context. Of the many general studies of Restoration theatre the introduction to the definitive but massive 'calendar', *The London Stage*, has helpfully been reprinted as a separate volume, *The London Stage 1660-1700: a Critical Introduction* by Emmett L. Avery and Arthur H. Scouten (Carbondale: Southern Illinois University Press, 1968), while the fifth volume of *The Revels History of Drama in English*, covering the period 1660 to 1750, edited by John Loftis and others (London: Methuen, 1976), usefully blends theatre history with dramatic criticism. But both volumes are, alas, typical in making only passing mention of Mrs. Behn – and Jocelyn Powell's *Restoration Theatre Practice* (London: Routledge, 1984), in all other respects an extremely valuable work, scarcely mentions our author. The full study of Aphra Behn's plays in their theatrical context remains to be written.

'She had been a Tory, a hedonist, a bohemian, and hardly, by the standards of the new generation, a lady. Gracefully, she didn't outlive her own.'

Robert Phelps (1950)

Critical Sidelights

'The morality of her plays is *au fond* that of many a comedy of to-day: that the situations and phrasing in which she presents her amorous intrigues and merry cuckoldoms do not conform with modern exposition of these themes we also show yet would not name, is but our surface gloss of verbal reticence; we hint, point, and suggest, where she spoke out broad words, frank and free; the *motif* is one and the same.'

Montague Summers (1915)

'Masterpieces are not single and solitary births; they are the outcome of many years of thinking in common, of thinking by the body of the people, so that the experience of the mass is behind the single voice. Jane Austen should have laid a wreath upon the grave of Fanny Burney, and George Eliot done homage to the robust shade of Eliza Carter. . . . All women together ought to let flowers fall upon the tomb of Aphra Behn . . . for it was she who earned them the right to speak their minds.'

Virginia Woolf (1929)

'Obviously, the best ingredient for guaranteeing the attention of a Restoration audience was sex. Politics was next best, but for a really sure-fire job it had better be sex. A play like *The Dutch Lover* (or any of Aphra's eighteen others) is not much else. Six couples *en mêle* for five acts. All the formulas and properties in the book are summoned up for duty: the bastard brother who really isn't a bastard; the younger sister who was fatally indiscreet; the maid who drops her mistress's key to the wrong swain; assignations in the woods; the girl disguised as a boy; the long-lost heir; somebody substituted for an expected guest; rakes, bosoms, trysts, masks, swords, honour, the all-important two thousand a year; one grand stew. But Aphra brings it off, neatly, easily, and at the final curtain everyone is happily bedded down.'

Robert Phelps (1950)

'Angellica, who has a complex literary ancestry extending far beyond *Thomaso*, does not quite fit the comic world of the play. She is a woman of the world, and certainly fair game for the Rover; Willmore does not deceive her with promises of marriage, and her experience is more than sufficient for her to recognise that his interest in her is ephemeral and purely sexual. Yet when she is deserted for Hellena, her sense of rejection and her understanding of her situation are so movingly presented as to take her for the moment out of the comic ethos entirely. She reappears, to be sure, as the traditional scorned woman seeking vengeance, but the shift from a believable and individualised woman to an artificial and conventional type is remarkably unconvincing.'

Frederick M. Link (1967)

'Mrs. Behn makes a splendidly representative dramatist for this period. She starts out with old-fashioned romantic tragicomedy, experiments with revenge tragedy, and moves with time into the sex comedy of the 1670s. During the Popish Plot, she turns political with her revision of *The Rump* and anti-Whig city comedy, and in one of her last comedies, *The Widow Ranter* (1969) we find her experimenting with an almost Drydenesque split tragicomedy. She never reached any heights of originality, but she eventually became a highly competent technician, turning out skilful exercises in contemporary drama.'

A.H. Scouten (1976)

'There were other voices who had begun to speak out against marriage-for-money in Aphra's time, but few took the logical conclusion of such a stance as far as she did, nor elaborated it as part of a larger politics of sexuality. Aphra was, though of course she did not know it, at the beginning of a 'sentimental revolution' that would eventually revise England's idea of marriage. Though it was clear Aphra's generation was witnessing a disintegration of the old form, the counsel Francis Osborne gave in his *Advice to a Son* (1656) was still uppermost in men's minds: "He that takes a wife wanting money is a slave to his affections, doing the basest of drudgeries without wages". Charles II confirmed this reality when, in 1664, he wrote to his sister that "a handsome face without money has but few gallants, upon the score of marriage".'

Angeline Goreau (1980)

'The imputation of plagiarism . . . was a minor theme in the diatribe against Aphra. The principal charge was that she had failed in feminine modesty – or as it was more commonly put, that she was a whore. . . . Wycherley nastily comments on her growing "public" fame – punning on the double sense of the word as it was applied to feminine sexuality at that time. . . . The logic Wycherley's joke rested on was well known to everyone: it was the old adage that in gaining "fame", a woman lost it.'

Angeline Goreau (1980)

Imogen Stubbs: GAOLER'S DAUGHTER

Hugh Quarshie: ARCITE

The Two Noble Kinsmen

Tony Church: OLD KNO'WELL

Henry Goodman: THOMAS KITELY

Every Man in His Humour

THE ROVER

APHRA BEHN

The Characters

In order of their appearance

FLORINDA		
VALERIA	}	three sisters
HELLENA		
DON PEDRO, their brother		
STEPHANO		
CALLIS	}	his servants
BELVILE, a Colonel		
FREDERICK, his friend		
BLUNT, a country gull	}	four come out of England
WILLMORE, the Rover		
LUCETTA, a whore		
SANCHO, her man		
ANGELLICA BIANCA, a famous courtesan		
MORETTA, her woman		
SEBASTIAN		
BISKEY	}	her bravos
DON ANTONIO, the viceroy's son		
DIEGO, his servant		
PHILIP, servant to the English		

Masquers, Servants, etc.

Scene: a colony of Spain, in Carnival time.

Director's Note

This is an adapted text. The original adaptation was made before rehearsals began, but it was much altered in the course of rehearsal. About 550 lines have been cut and some 350 added.

Many of the new lines are taken from an earlier source play which Aphra Behn herself used extensively when she wrote *The Rover*. This is *Thomaso* or *The Wanderer* by Thomas Killigrew, published in 1664. Aphra Behn took over many of its situations, characters and lines, sometimes word for word. Though *The Rover* is a far better play, it is hazy and loose in places, and *Thomaso* has the edge at specific moments.

The alterations I have made are partly to streamline our version and help to clarify a confusing plot. The most obvious change is the turning of Belvile into a black soldier of fortune, and the setting of the play in a Spanish colony rather than in Spain. I have however, deliberately avoided naming a specific location. The most obvious addition is that Valeria is introduced earlier in the action. Aphra Behn seems to regard her as an important engine of the plot, but does not have her speak until well into the play. The scene between Blunt and Lucetta is now closer to *Thomaso* than *The Rover*, Angellica's part has been expanded in the first half, as have the parts of Sebastian, Biskey and Sancho. And there are a number of substantial transpositions, particularly in the first four scenes.

John Barton
Stratford, November 1986

Scene i

A chamber with a chest in it.
Enter Florinda, Valeria and Hellena.

FLORINDA.

What an impertinent thing is a young girl bred in a nunnery! How full of questions! Prithee no more, Hellena; I have told thee more than thou understand'st already.

HELLENA.

The more's my grief. I would fain know as much as you, which makes me so inquisitive; (*Florinda sighs*) Nor is't enough I know you're a lover, unless you tell me to who 'tis you sigh for

FLORINDA.

When you're a lover I'll think you fit for a secret of that nature.

HELLENA.

'Tis true, I never was a lover yet, but I begin to have a shrewd guess what 'tis to be so, and fancy it very pretty to sigh, and sing, and blush, and wish, and long and wish to see the man, and when I do, look pale and tremble, just as you did when my brother brought home the fine colonel from England to see you. What do you call him Florinda? Belvile?

FLORINDA.

Fie, Hellena.

HELLENA.

. . . Or is it Don Antonio the Viceroy's son? Or perhaps the rich old Don Vincentio, whom my father designs you for a husband? Why do you blush?

FLORINDA.

With indignation. . . . I shall let my father see I understand better what's due to my beauty, birth, and fortune, and more to my soul . . .

HELLENA.

Now hang me, if I don't love thee for that dear disobedience. I love mischief strangely, as most of our sex do. . . . But tell me, Florinda, don't you love that fine Belvile? . . .

FLORINDA.

Hellena, a maid designed for a nun ought not to be so curious in a discourse of love.

HELLENA.

And dost thou think that ever I'll be a nun?

VALERIA.   Yes!
FLORINDA.

HELLENA.

Or at least till I'm so old I'm fit for nothing else? . . . Prithee tell me, what does thou see about me that is unfit for love? Have I not a world of youth? A humour gay? A beauty passable? A vigour desirable? Well shaped? Clean limbed? Sweet breathed? And sense enough to know how all these ought to be employed to the best advantage? Yes, I do and will.

FLORINDA.

Prithee be not so wild.

VALERIA.

But tell us, Florinda, how you came acquainted with this Belvile, for I perceive you knew him before we came here.

FLORINDA.

Yes, I knew him in Spain at the siege of Pamplona; he was then a colonel of French horse, who when the town was ransacked, nobly treated our brother Pedro and myself.

HELLENA.

Was he not born in this place?

FLORINDA.

Yes, and went hence to make his fortune. He was in England in the wars and was a cavalier with good King Charles. But when the King was headed he turned mercenary and was in France and Spain and Flanders. And now he is come home with's English friends to see the Carnival.

HELLENA.

And thee, I warrant.

FLORINDA.

I must own, I have I know not what that pleads kindly for him about my heart.

HELLENA.

(*to Valeria*). And you, sister mouse? How goes it with thine?

VALERIA.

It hath a kind of carnival beating. And though I prattle not so much as you, sisters, my mind's as busy as both of you together. When our brother is gone out in's finery, I have a device to unfold.

STEPHANO.

Madam your brother comes.

Enter Don Pedro and Callis.

PEDRO.

Good morrow, sister. Florinda, pray when saw you your lover Don Vicentio?

FLORINDA.

I know not, sir. Callis, when was he here? For I consider it so little I know not when it was.

PEDRO.

I have a command from my father to tell you you ought not to despise a man of so vast a fortune. and such a passion for you. (*Puts on his masking habit.*)

FLORINDA.

A passion for me? 'Tis more than e'er I saw. I hate Vincentio, sir, and I would not have a man so dear to me as my brother follow the ill customs of our country and make a slave of his sister. Oh, sweet Pedro, my father's will I'm sure you may divert.

PEDRO.

I know not how dear I am to you, but I wish only to be ranked in your esteem equal with my friend Colonel Belvile. Why do you frown and blush? Is there any guilt belongs to the name of that cavalier?

FLORINDA.

I'll not deny I value Belvile. And will you not allow him my esteem?

PEDRO.

Yes, pay him what you will in honour, as I do, but you must consider Don Vincentio's fortune, and the jointure he'll make you.

FLORINDA.

Let him consider my youth, beauty, and fortune, which ought not to be thrown away on his age and jointure.

PEDRO.

'Tis true, he's not so young and fine a gentleman as that Belvile. But what jewels will that cavalier present you with? Those of his eyes and heart?

HELLENA.

And are not those better than any Don Vincentio has here in the Indies?

PEDRO.

. . . Go, Hellena! Up to your devotion? You are not designed for the conversation of lovers.

HELLENA

(*aside*). Nor saints yet a while, I hope. – Is't not enough you make a nun of me, but you must cast my sister away too, exposing her to a worse confinement than a religious life?

PEDRO.

Is it a confinement to be carried into the country to a rich villa with a fine air, large fields, and gardens where she may walk and gather flowers?

HELLENA.

And if these be her daily divertissements, what are those of the night? To lie in a wide moth-eaten bedchamber and there the old giant uncases his feeble carcass, stretches himself, sighs a belch or two, stales in your pot, farts loud as a musket, throws himself into bed and expects you in his foul sheets . . .

PEDRO.

Have you done yet?

HELLENA.

And this man you must kiss and nuzzle through his beard to find his lips. And this you must submit to for threescore years . . .

PEDRO.

For all your character of Don Vincentio, she is as like to marry him as she was before.

HELLENA.

Marry Don Vincentio? Hang me, such a wedlock would be worse than adultery with another man.

PEDRO.

Callis, take her hence and lock her up all this Carnival, and at Lent, at the end of the week, she shall begin her everlasting penance in a nunnery.

HELLENA

(*aside*). Shall I so? I am like to make a fine nun! I have an excellent humour for a cloister!

PEDRO.

Callis, make it your business to watch this wildcat. Fie, you're a troublesome pair to me. I would ye were both as modest as your sister Valeria is. – But for you, Florinda, I've only tried you all this while and urged my father's will. But mine is that you would love Antonio the Viceroy's son: he is brave and young, and all that can complete the happiness of a gallant maid. . . . My father's absence will give us opportunity to free you from Vincentio by marrying here, which you must do tomorrow.

FLORINDA.

Tomorrow!

PEDRO.

Tomorrow, before my father returns, or 'twill be too late. 'Tis not only my friendship to Antonio which makes me urge this, but love to thee; therefore thou shalt stay here in thy chamber and resolve upon tomorrow.

FLORINDA.
Sir, I shall strive to do as shall become your sister.

PEDRO.
I'll both believe and trust you. Callis, look to it. Adieu.

Exit Pedro.

HELLENA.
As becomes his sister! That is to be resolved your way as he is his. But hark you, Callis, you will not be so cruel as to lock us up indeed, will you?

CALLIS.
I must obey the commands I have.

HELLENA.
Oh, Callis . . .

FLORINDA.
I ne'er till now perceived my ruin near.
I've no defence against Antonio's love,
For he has all the advantages of nature,
Both youth and fortune, and his power i'this place.

VALERIA.
You have a defence, Florinda.

FLORINDA.
I've none. I am ruined.

VALERIA.
Fie, how dull you are. If you will marry Belvile within these two days, neither our brother nor our father can compel you to another. 'Tis palpable.

CALLIS.
Nay, she shall not.

FLORINDA.
But how? I am pent up and have no access to him.

VALERIA.
You shall have if I may rule you. If you would have man, you must win man, and be a little wanton ere ye be won. And therefore you must seek him out, and go disguised lest our brother spy you.

FLORINDA.
I dare not.

CALLIS.
Nor is it fitting –

VALERIA.
Nay, listen. I have guises in this chest should serve for all of us to go together. (*To Callis.*) Yes, and you likewise.

CALLIS.
Me?

FLORINDA.
We dare not be so free.

VALERIA.
Why think you there be Carnivals, but that men, and women too, may be as free as they *will* ere Lent be come? Nay, dally not!

CALLIS.
You may not.

VALERIA
(*undressing*). Hellena, here's stuff for you.

FLORINDA.
If Belvile sees me in a guise, he'll think me too free.

VALERIA.
Nay, you must woo him in semblance of your new person, that at first he may not know you.

FLORINDA.
How?

VALERIA.
Must I expound to you the very pith of Carnival? Why think you our brother Pedro has gone thither? To lie with wenches.

HELLENA.
No!

VALERIA.
And why in so fantastic and lusty a guise? To maintain his sober reputation to the world. Have not I heard thee say women should do as men do? Florinda, undress you straight!

CALLIS.
Valeria, nay, they shall not.

HELLENA.
Sweet Callis, sweet, sweet Callis –

CALLIS.
What, go in masquerade? 'Twill be a fine farewell to the world, I take it, What would you do there?

HELLENA.
That which all the world does and take all innocent freedoms. (*Undresses.*) We'll all go together.

VALERIA.

Put off this moping humour with your clothes, Florinda. Shall Pedro frolic and leave us three mewed up?

FLORINDA.

Nay then, we will, but to spite our brother. Callis, will you give us leave to go and try your future too?

CALLIS.

Faith, I have an itch of going. If I thought your brother might not know it, and I might wait on you –

She and Callis undress.

HELLENA

(*to Callis*). Thou shalt attend and watch us.

VALERIA.

Then put this and this on.

FLORINDA.

What wanton gear is this?

VALERIA.

We shall go as gypsies.

FLORINDA.

I shall be bashful and know not what to say.

VALERIA.

Fie, be that which I know you inly are. If wenches must needs be demure and nice year in and out, 'tis fit they should be free and frolic for one week in the calendar.

CALLIS.

For as 'tis true, all men are stark mad for wenches, so 'tis true, however custom pretends otherwise, that we wenches be as inly stark as men.

Music without.

VALERIA.

Hark, it begins.

HELLENA.

Now have I rare itch to dance and to lure fellows.

FLORINDA.

Who will like thee well enough to have thee, that sees what a mad wench thou art?

HELLENA.

Like me? I don't intend every he that likes me shall have me, but he that I like. I should have stayed in the nunnery still if I had liked my lady abbess as well as she liked me. No, I came thence not, as my wise brother imagines, to take an eternal farewell of the world, but to love and to be beloved; and I will be beloved, or I'll get one of your men, so I will.

VALERIA.

Am I put into the number of lovers?

HELLENA.

You? Why, sister, I know thou'rt as hot within as any lady in the Indies.

VALERIA.

Then let's vie with one another who shall first win her man.

FLORINDA.

I'll write a note ere we go, and if I chance to see Belvile, although he will not know me, I'll give it him to let him know Florinda favours him. Yea, and I'll give him too all the letters I have writ but dared not send for fear of my brother.

VALERIA.

Haste, haste.

CALLIS.

Hark how gay it sounds.

FLORINDA.

Fie, Valeria, thou look'st too wanton.

VALERIA.

Why so I am, and will be!

HELLENA.

Let's go.

CALLIS.

Now St. Jago, that is patron of Carnival, smile on our devising!

FLORINDA.

Why then, lead on. Though I be shamed or shent
I'll try my fortune too ere it be Lent!

They go forth into the street and flaunt at diverse Masquers, that are all fantastically dressed. They dance and then run out, the Masquers following.

Scene ii

A long street.
Enter diverse people who dress for Carnival.
Enter Belvile, melancholy, Blunt and Frederick following.

FREDERICK.

Colonel! Why, what the devil ails thee colonel, in a time when all the world is gay to look like mere Lent thus? Hadst thou been here long enough to have been in love, I should have sworn some such judgement had befallen thee.

BELVILE.
No, I have made no new amours since I came home.

FREDERICK.
You have left none behind you in Paris?

BELVILE.
Neither.

FREDERICK.
I cannot divine the cause then, unless the old cause, the want of money.

BLUNT.
And another old cause, the want of a wench. Would not that revive you?

BELVILE.
You are mistaken, Ned.

BLUNT.
Nay, 'adsheartlikins, then thou'rt past cure.

FREDERICK.
I have found it out: thou hast brought us here to pursue thy acquaintance with the lady that cost thee so many sighs at the siege of Pamplona – pox on't, what d'ye call her – . . . Florinda. Ay, Florinda. And will nothing serve thy turn but that damned, virtuous woman, whom on my conscience thou lov'st in spite too, because thou seest little or no possibility of gaining her?

BELVILE.
Thou art mistaken Fred; I have int'rest enough in that lovely virgin's heart to make me proud and vain, were it not abated by the severity of her brother Pedro, who, perceiving my happiness –

FREDERICK.
Has civilly forbid thee the house?

BELVILE.
'Tis so, to make way for a powerful rival, Don Antonio, the Viceroy's son, who has the advantage of me in being a man of fortune, a noble Spaniard, and her brother's friend; which gives him liberty to make his court, whilst I have recourse only to letters and distant looks from her window . . .

BLUNT.
Heyday! What the devil are we made of that we cannot be thus concerned for a wench?

FREDERICK.
I dare swear I have had a hundred as young, kind and handsome as this Florinda; and dogs eat me if they were not as troublesome to me i'th' morning as they were welcome o'er night.

BLUNT.
And yet I warrant he would not touch another woman if he might have her for nothing.

BELVILE.
That's thy joy, a cheap whore.

BLUNT.
'Adsheartlikins, when did you ever hear of an honest woman that took a man's money? Yet you cavaliers have been kept so poor with Parliaments and Protectors the little stock you have is not worth preserving. But I thank my stars I had more grace than to forfeit my estate as Fred has, by cavaliering.

Enter Willmore

BELVILE.
Willmore!

WILLMORE.
Ha! Dear Belvile! Noble colonel!

BLUNT.
Willmore! Welcome ashore, my dear rover! What happy wind blew us this good fortune?

WILLMORE.
Let me salute my dear Fred, and then command me. – How is't, honest lad?

FREDERICK.
Faith, sir, the old compliment, infinitely the better to see my dear mad Willmore again. Prithee, why camst thou ashore?

WILLMORE.
My business ashore is only to enjoy myself a little this Carnival. I must aboard again in a day or two.

FREDERICK.
And where's the Prince?

WILLMORE.
He's well, and reigns still lord of the wat'ry element.

A toast.

ALL.
The Prince!

BELVILE.

Pray know our new friend, sir; he's a raw traveller, but honest, stout, and one of us. (*Embraces Blunt.*)

WILLMORE.

That you esteem him gives him an int'rest here.

BLUNT.

Your servant, sir. I am a country gentleman from Essex.

WILLMORE.

But well, faith. I'm glad to meet you again in a warm climate, where the kind sun has a godlike power still over the wine and women. Love and mirth are my business here.

FREDERICK.

No friend to love like a long voyage at sea.

BLUNT.

Except a nunnery.

FREDERICK.

Now for some plump girl, flat noses for convenience of kissing, with some brave swelled lips, soft and sweet; their very sweat's balsam in the dog days.

Enter several Men in masking habits, some playing on music, others dancing after; Women dressed like courtesans, with papers pinned on their breasts, and baskets of flowers in their hands.

BELVILE.

See, here be those kind merchants of love you look for.

BLUNT.

'Adsheartlikins, what have we here?

FREDERICK.

Now the game begins. How they eye us!

WILLMORE.

Fine pretty creatures! What's here? May a stranger have leave to look and love? 'Roses for every month'? (*Reads the papers.*)

BLUNT.

Roses for every month? What means that?

BELVILE.

They are, or would have you think they're courtesans, who here are to be hired by the month.

WILLMORE.

Kind and obliging to inform us.

BELVILE.

You must need have a care lest ye be gulled.

WILLMORE.

Pray where do these roses grow? I would fain plant some of 'em in a bed of mine.

BELVILE.

Thou has need of such a remedy for thou stink'st of tar and ropes' ends like a dock or pesthouse.

WOMAN.

Beware such roses, sir.

WILLMORE.

A pox of fear . . . Death, will you not be kind? Quickly be kind?

The woman puts herself into the hands of a man and exeunt.

BELVILE.

By no means use violence here in Carnival time. I would not have you at your old tricks here in the place that I was bred.

WILLMORE.

Death! Just as I was going to be damnably in love, to have her led off!

FREDERICK.

Let's find some other game.

BELVILE.

Yea but, first you must disguise and muzzle yourself as we have done.

WILLMORE.

Why?

BELVILE.

Because whatever extravagances we commit in maskers' faces, our own may not be obliged to answer them.

WILLMORE.

I'll not change my eternal buff.

FREDERICK.

Nay, you must prank yourself up a little like the rest, for 'tis Carnival and 'tis in honour of our colonel who's come home.

They get gear and masks.

Song.

Sancho and Lucetta come forward.

SANCHO.

These be good game.

LUCETTA.

And strangers too; I know it by their gazing. They're English too, and they say that's a sort of goodnatured loving people, that have generally so kind an opinion of themselves that a woman with any wit may flatter 'em into any sort of fool she pleases.

SANCHO.

Nay, mark yon bumpkin that roars the loudest. When did I mistake your game? Go to it.

LUCETTA.

Nay, Sancho –

SANCHO.

Go, or I'll beat thee. Yet, mark. You shall promise much, but pay him little.

LUCETTA.

Fie on your jealous humour. If I understand my trade, he's mine. (*Calls*) 'Roses for every month!'

She passes by Blunt and gazes on him. He struts and cocks and gazes likewise.

BLUNT.

So, she's taken. I have beauties which my glass at home did not discover.

> *Lucetta goes out, Blunt and Sancho following.*
> *Belvile, Frederick and Willmore come forward with Carnival caps and vizard.*

WILLMORE.

What, is this Essex calf the first of us to raise a she hare?

FREDERICK.

I hope 'tis some common crafty sinner, that will sell him for Peru: the rogue's sturdy, and would work well in a mine.

BELVILE.

A pox upon him . . . he's our banker, and has all our cash about him; and if he fail, we are all broke.

FREDERICK.

Oh, let him alone for that matter; he's of a damned stingy quality that will secure our stock, otherwise, if he part with more than a piece of eight, geld him . . .

WILLMORE.

Prithee what humour is he of, that you wish him so well?

BELVILE.

One that knows no pleasure beyond riding to the next fair.

FREDERICK.

Educated in a nursery, with a maid to tend him till fifteen.

WILLMORE.

'Tis a lucky devil to light upon so kind a wench! Oh, for my arms full of white, kind woman.

> *They exit.*

Scene iii

The street.
Enter Willmore, Belvile and Frederick, Florinda, Valeria and Hellena, dressed as gypsies, Callis following.

HELLENA.

Sister, there's your colonel.

VALERIA.

And with him two proper fellows.

CALLIS

(*aside*). Nay, have a care, The devil's in those English when they go abroad.

FREDERICK.

Ha, gypsies, on my life! To them!

VALERIA.

To them!

HELLENA.

Callis, do you the like.

WILLMORE.

There's a likely wench. Would I could drop an anchor in your cove!

HELLENA

(*aside*). Yonder in buff's a proper fellow. I'll to him, and instead of telling his fortune, try my own. (*She advances on Willmore.*)

WILLMORE.

Dear, pretty, and I hope, young devil, will you tell an amorous stranger what luck he's like to have?

HELLENA.

Have a care how you venture with me, sir, lest I pick your pocket, which will more vex your English humour than a Spanish fortune will please you.

WILLMORE.

How the devil cam'st thou to know my country and humour?

HELLENA.

The first I guess by a certain forward impudence, which does not displease me at this time; and the loss of your money will vex you because I guess you have but very little to lose.

WILLMORE.

Egad, child, thou'rt i'th' right. It is so little, I dare not offer it thee for a kindness. . . . But cannot you divine what other things I have about me that I would more willingly part with?

HELLENA.

Indeed no, that's the business of a witch, and I am but a gypsy yet. Yet without looking in your hand, I have a parlous guess 'tis some foolish heart you mean, an inconstant English heart, as little worth stealing as your purse.

They withdraw.
Florinda and Belvile come forward, the other pairs retiring.

FLORINDA

(*aside*). Alas, Callis, watches me so, I dare not discover myself. Yet I'll assay. (*To Belvile*) Sir, by this line you should be a lover. (*Looking in his hand.*)

BELVILE.

Come, let me go; I'm weary of this fooling.

FLORINDA.

I will not sir, till you have confessed whether the passion that you have vowed Florinda be true or false. (*She holds him; he strives to get from her.*)

BELVILE.

Florinda!

FLORINDA.

Softly.

BELVILE.

Thou hast nam'd one will fix me here forever.

FLORINDA.

She'll be disappointed then, who expects you this night at the garden gate. And if you fail not, as – (*looks on Callis, who observes 'em*) – Let me see the other hand – you will go near to do, she vows to die or make you happy.

BELVILE.

What canst thou mean?

FLORINDA.

That which I say.

CALLIS.

Madam, beware your brother.

FLORINDA.

Farewell. (*Offers to go.*)

BELVILE.

Oh charming sybil, stay; complete that joy which as it is will turn into distraction! Where must I be? At the garden gate? At night, you say?

CALLIS.

Madam, beware your brother.

FLORINDA.

Take these to instruct you farther. (*Gives him letters.*)

FREDERICK.

Have a care, sir, what you promise; this may be a trap to ruin you.

BELVILE.

Do not disturb my happiness with doubts.

VALERIA

(*to Frederick*). I see, sir, you mean to ruin me. And so you shall, if once you catch me.

She runs off, Frederick following; Belvile opens the letter and retires.

CALLIS.

Lo, all three have got a man already. I'll not dress thus if I go with them again for very shame no fellow takes me also. And yet I see that women may do most of their business on earth themselves, if they would but leave their spinning and try. Then if I did not fear my master's anger, I might assay and get some spicey fellow if once I spyed one. For I am as eager within as any wench in the Indies. (*Sees Hellena approach.*) O fie, is this she that is to be a nun? (*Withdraws.*)

Re-enter Willmore and Hellena.

HELLENA.

If you should prevail with my tender heart, as I begin to fear you will, for you have horrible loving eyes, there will be difficulty in't that you'll hardly undergo for my sake,

WILLMORE.

Faith, child, I have been bred in dangers. . . . Let it be anything but a long siege, and I'll undertake it.

HELLENA.

Can you storm?

WILLMORE.

Oh, most furiously.

HELLENA.

What think you of a nunnery wall? For he that wins me must gain that first.

WILLMORE.

A nun! Oh now I love thee for't! There's no sinner like a young saint. Nay, now there's no denying me; the old law had no curse to a woman like dying a maid: witness Jeptha's daughter.

HELLENA.

A good text this, if well-handled; I perceive, good Father Captain, you design only to make me fit for heaven, which will grieve me for, when I begin, I fancy I shall love like anything; I never tried yet.

WILLMORE.

Egad, and that's kind! Prithee, dear creature, give me credit for a heart, for faith, I'm a very honest fellow. Oh, I long to come first to the banquet of love! And such a swinging appetite I bring. Oh, I'm impatient. Thy lodging, sweetheart, thy lodging, or I'm a dead man!

HELLENA.

Why must we be either guilty of fornication or murder if we converse with you men? Is there no difference between leave to love me, and leave to lie with me?

WILLMORE.

Faith, child, they were made to go together.

HELLENA.

Nay, canst thou prove that?

WILLMORE.

Try me.

HELLENA.

So I mean to. If you will meet me in this place after dinner . . .

WILLMORE.

Yea, what then?

HELLENA.

And if you will swear to keep your heart and not bestow it between this and that.

WILLMORE.

By all the little gods of love, I swear it. I'll leave it with you.

HELLENA.

Then it is possible that I may see you.

Enter Florinda and Valeria.

FLORINDA.

Away, away! Sister, our brother comes.

VALERIA.

Up with your masks! All's well. Our men are hooked.

HELLENA.

Yea, the field's ours.

VALERIA.

I warrant you, we've thumped them.

They go.

Enter Frederick.

FREDERICK.

Thou hadst a great deal of talk with thy little gypsy; couldst thou do no good upon her? Mine was hardhearted.

WILLMORE.

Hang her, she was some damned honest person of quality. I'm sure, she was so very free and witty. Pray heaven, if ever I do see her again, she prove damnably ugly, that I may fortify myself against her tongue.

FREDERICK.

Have a care of love, for o' my conscience she was not of a quality to give thee any hopes.

WILLMORE.

Pox on 'em, why do they draw a man in then? She has played with my heart so, that 'twill never lie still till I have met with some kind wench that will play the game out with me.

BELVILE

(*entering*). Oh friends, the welcom'st news! The softest letters! Nay, you shall all see them!

WILLMORE.

The reason of this mighty joy?

BELVILE.

'Tis Florinda's hand!
All blessings fall upon the virtuous maid.

FREDERICK.

Nay, no idolatory; a sober sacrifice I'll allow you.

BELVILE.

See how kindly she invites me to deliver her from the threatened violence of her brother. Will you not assist me?

WILLMORE.

I know not what thou mean'st, but I'll make one at any mischief where a woman's concerned. But she'll be grateful to us for the favour, will she not?

BELVILE.

How mean you?

WILLMORE.

How should I mean? Thou know'st there's but one way for a woman to oblige me.

BELVILE.

Do not profane; the maid is nicely virtuous.

WILLMORE.

Why, pox, then she's fit for nothing but a husband. Let her e'en go, colonel.

FREDERICK.

Peace, she's the colonel's mistress, sir.

WILLMORE.

Nay, then let her be the devil, if she be thy mistress I'll serve her. Name the way.

BELVILE.

Read here this postscript. (*Gives him the letter.*)

WILLMORE

(*reads*). 'At ten at night, at the garden gate, of which, if I cannot get the key, I will contrive a way over the wall. Come attended with a friend or two.' – Kind heart, if we three cannot weave a string to let her down a garden wall, 'twere pity but the hangman wove one for us all.

FREDERICK.

Let her alone for that; your woman's wit, your fair kind woman, will out-trick a broker or a Jew.

Scene iv

The same.
Enter Blunt.

BLUNT.

Colonel, I have been an ass, a deluded fool, a very coxcomb from my birth till this hour, and heartily repent my little faith.

BELVILE.

What the devil's the matter with thee, Ned?

BLUNT.

Oh, such a mistress, Fred! Such a girl!

WILLMORE.

Ha! where?

FREDERICK.

Ay, Where?

BLUNT.

So fond, so amorous, so toying, and so fine! And all for sheer love, ye rogue!

WILLMORE.

Death, Man, where is she?

BLUNT.

Oh how she looked and kissed! I never tasted such a melting snowy girl. Fred, try if she has not left the taste of her balmy kisses upon my lips. (*Kisses him. Belvile laughs.*) How have I laughed at the colonel when he sighed for love! But now the little archer has revenged him! . . . Well, I'm resolved to sell all in Essex and plant here forever . . .

WILLMORE.

Dost know her name?

BLUNT.

Her name? No, 'adsheartlikins. What care I for names? She's fair, young, brisk and kind, even to ravishment! . . .

FREDERICK.

Didst give her anything?

BLUNT.

Give her? Ha! Ha! Ha! She's a person of quality. Dost think such creatures are to be bought? 'Adsheartlikins, she presented me with this bracelet for the toy of a diamond I used to wear. Ned Blunt's not everybody. She expects me again tonight.

WILLMORE.

Egad, that's well; we'll all go.

BLUNT.

No, gentleman, not a soul. 'Adsheartlikins, you're all fools. There are things about this Essex calf that shall take with the ladies, beyond all your wit and parts. This shape and size, gentlemen, are not to be despised, my waist, too, tolerably long, with other inviting signs that shall be nameless.

FREDERICK.

Well, sir, for all your nameless inviting signs, I shall be very glad to understand your purse be secure; 'tis our whole estate at present.

BELVILE.

But didst thou give her a diamond, say you?

FREDERICK.

A pox, Ned 'tis some common whore, upon my life.

BLUNT.

A whore? Yes, with such clothes, and so attended! A whore!

BELVILE.

Why yes, sir, they are all whores, – I know this place – whores in gay clothes and bright jewels; whores with great houses richly furnished with velvet beds, store of plate, handsome attendance, and fine coaches; all whores, and errant ones.

WILLMORE.

Pox on't, where do these fine whores live?

BELVILE.

I'll advise thee.

Enter two Bravos, Sebastian and Biskey, and hang up a great picture of Angellica against the balcony.

One lives near by

FREDERICK.

The famous Castilliana, Angellica Bianca.

BELVILE.

See, there, the fair sign to the inn where a man may lodge that's fool enough to give her price.

BLUNT.

'Adsheartlikins, gentlemen, what's this?

BELVILE.

A famous Spanish courtesan, that's to be sold.

BLUNT.

How? To be sold? Nay, then I have nothing to say to her. Sold? What impudence is practised in this country. Come, let's be gone; I'm sure we're no buyers of this commodity.

FREDERICK.

Thou art none, I'm sure, unless thou couldst have her in thy bed at a price of a coach in the street.

WILLMORE.

How wondrous fair she is! A thousand crowns a month? By heaven, as many kingdoms were too little! A plague of this poverty, of which I ne'er complain but when it hinders my approach to beauty which virtue ne'er could purchase. (*Turns from the picture.*)

BLUNT.

What's this? (*Reads.*) 'A thousand crowns a month'! 'Adsheartlikins, here's a sum! Sure 'tis a mistake. – (*To one of the Bravos.*) Hark you, friend, does she take or give so much by the month?

FREDERICK.

A thousand crowns! Why, 'tis a portion for the Infanta!

BLUNT.

Hark ye friends, won't she trust?

SEBASTIAN.

This is a trade, sir that cannot live by credit.

BLUNT.

Come, gentlemen, let's be gone to dinner.

FREDERICK.

Let's get a wench first; some dainty plantation sinner.

BELVILE.

Yea, after dinner we'll pass the day as you please. But at night ye must all be at my devotion. For then, I mean to meet Florinda at the garden gate.

FREDERICK.

We will not fail you.

WILLMORE

(*gazing at Angellica's picture as he goes*). I long to see the shadow of that fair substance.

They go.

Scene v

The same.
The bravos sitting before Angellica's picture.

SEBASTIAN.

'Tis my opinion this bait will catch no fish. I'd be loath my wages should be deducted out of the first fruits of so mad a project.

BISKEY.

Sure, 'tis a dull trade to sit here watching of shadows. Methinks we would have got more in a booth with a picture of an elephant for two pence a piece.

SEBASTIAN.

Yet 'tis better than chewing cane on the plantations.

BISKEY.

Yea, and since we're hired for the time of Carnival, and since we're well paid for it, let us enjoy the time.

SEBASTIAN.

So I mean to. Yet, a pox on this Spanish avarice that knows not how to enjoy their Indies to the right use.

MORETTA.

You're vexed to find the trade so refined here by a stranger.

ANGELLICA.

Sebastian!

MORETTA.

My mistress calls you.

BISKEY.

Peace, she comes.

SEBASTIAN.

Well, let's praise her still. For vain women are ships that sail only with windy flattery.

MORETTA.

Make haste you Rogues. Pox on these galley slaves. We should have brought our own bravos from Spain.

ANGELLICA.

(to the bravos). Prithee, what said all those fellows to thee that have been here today?

SEBASTIAN.

Nay, they were admirers of beauty only, but no purchasers.

BISKEY.

They were merry with your price and picture, laughed at the sum, and so passed off.

ANGELLICA.

No matter, I'm not displeased with their rallying.

SEBASTIAN.

Yet, one I knew, through all his disguises, to be Don Pedro, nephew to the general, and who was with him in Pamplona.

ANGELLICA.

Don Pedro? My general's nephew? When the old gallant died, he left him a vast sum of money. Don Pedro! It is he who was so in love with me in Spain, and made the old general so jealous.

MORETTA.

If I am not mistaken, he is the likeliest man to pay your price.

ANGELLICA.

Nay, he's of a humour so uneasy and inconstant that the victory over his heart is as soon lost as won . . . But inconstancy's the sin of all mankind, therefore I'm resolved that nothing but more gold shall ever charm my heart.

MORETTA.

I'm glad on't, 'tis only interest women of our profession ought to consider, but muse still what has kept you from that general disease of our sex so long; I mean that of being in love.

ANGELLICA.

A kind but sullen star under which I had the happiness to be born. Nay, I've had no time for love. I have been too busy winning admiration. I thank my star I have longed for no man yet. What need I, since all I see are offered before I ask? I have refused many but never yet desired one.

MORETTA.

Yet, thou hast enjoyed many.

ANGELLICA.

Yea, but they purchased me at a golden rate.

MORETTA.

Would we were back in Spain again. What needs this Carnival trick? You have youth and future to spare, and may look about and choose your men at leisure.

ANGELLICA.

I would not stay one month longer in this town, Moretta, but for the vanity and pleasure to see and to be seen. While the old general lived, his jealousy kept me dead to the world, neither seen or enjoyed. But I'll seek my pleasure now and leave a name and memory behind me. I know there's few are like to give the money; nor want I any neither. Yet I'll have the gusto to see them gaze and sigh and wish for what they may not have. And when our nine days' wonder's over, we'll be gone. Nay, I would eat bran ere any he in breeches in this place should come between my sheets.

Music.

SEBASTIAN.

Here's Don Pedro again.

MORETTA.

And there's Antonio, the Viceroy's son.

ANGELLICA.

I'll fetch my lute, for 'tis for one of these that I have spread my nets.

They go in.

Scene vi

Martial music. Enter Don Pedro and Stephano at one door, and Don Antonio and Diego, his page, at another; all in masquerade. They go up to the picture.

ANTONIO.
A thousand crowns! Had not the painter flattered her, I should not think it dear.

PEDRO.
(aside to Stephano). Flattered her? By heaven, he cannot. I have seen the original, nor is there one charm here more than adorns her face and eyes; all this soft and sweet, with a certain languishing air that no artist can represent.

ANTONIO.
'Tis an excellent picture; whose hand can it be?

SEBASTIAN.
Van Dyke's.

ANTONIO.
'Tis well done.

SEBASTIAN.
He was a great master and a civil pencil.

ANTONIO.
(to Diego). What I heard of her beauty before had fired my soul, but this confirmation of it has blown it to a flame.

PEDRO.
Ha!

DIEGO.
Sir, I have known you throw away a thousand crowns on a worse face, and though you are near your marriage, you may venture a little love here; Florinda will not miss it.

PEDRO
(aside). Ha! Florinda! Sure 'tis Antonio.

ANTONIO.
Florinda! Name not those distant joys, there's not one thought of her will check my passion here. Fetch me a thousand crowns.

Diego goes.

PEDRO.
(aside). Florinda scorned! And all my hopes defeated of the possession of Angellica! *(Antonio gazes up.)* I'll give her a thousand crowns ere his be fetched.

Exit Stephano.

ANTONIO.
(to the bravos). Friends, where must I pay my off'ring of love? It's my thousand crowns I mean.

PEDRO.
That off'ring, sir, I have designed to make
And yours will come too late. Prithee, begone.

ANTONIO.
(aside). Who should this rival be?
Sirrah, go hence; I shall grow angry else,
And then thou art not safe.

PEDRO.
My anger may be fatal, sir, as yours,
And he that enters here may prove this truth.

ANTONIO.
I know not who thou art, but I am sure thou'rt worth my killing, for aiming at Angellica.

They draw and fight. Enter Willmore, Blunt and Frederick.

BLUNT.
'Adsheartlikins, here's fine doings.

FREDERICK.
Tilting for the wench, I'm sure.

WILLMORE.
Nay, gad, if swords will win her we have as good as the best of them. Put up, put up, and take another time and place, for this is designed for lovers only.

The English attack and disarm the Spaniards.

ANTONIO.
We are prevented.

PEDRO.
But by whom I know not.
Durst meet tomorrow morning on the Molo?
For I've a title to a better quarrel,
That of Florinda, in whose credulous heart
Thou'st made an int'rest, and destroyed my hopes.

ANTONIO.
Dare! Yea, for her or for Angellica
I'll meet thee there as early as the day.

PEDRO.

Then let us both come there disguised again,
That whosoever chance to get the better
May escape unknown.

ANTONIO.   'Tis well. It shall be so.

WILLMORE.
This posture's loose and negligent;
The sight on't would beget a warm desire
In souls whom impotence and age had chilled,
This must along with us.

Willmore fires a pistol at the picture. It hangs askew.

ANTONIO.
What means this rudeness, sir? Restore the picture.

PEDRO.
Ha! Rudeness committed to the fair Angellica! Restore the picture, sir.

WILLMORE.   Nay, I will not, sir.

ANTONIO.
By heaven, you shall.

WILLMORE.
Nay, show no swords again,
For if you do, I swear by this dear beauty,
I'll show mine too.

PEDRO.   What right can you pretend?

WILLMORE.
That of possession, sir, which I will maintain. You, perhaps, have a thousand crowns to give for the original.

PEDRO.
These be the English rogues that are hither come.

BLUNT.
Yea, by King Charles.

ANTONIO.
These be the oaken rogues; all rogues and rovers.

PEDRO.
What, will you fight upon as little reason
As you are wont to love?

WILLMORE.   Yea, and as hot.

FREDERICK.
And in good Prince Rupert's vein.

ANTONIO.
What, not content with civil broils at home,
But you must needs abuse us in the Indies?

PEDRO.
Let's teach them, sir, what 'tis to fire a flintlock

When it is Carnival. Let's join and thwack them.

ANTONIO.
'Tis well; and yet I'll meet with you tomorrow. (*To Willmore*)
Restore the picture, sir, or leave your lives behind.

BLUNT.
Death! You lie.

WILLMORE.   We will do neither.

They fight. The Spaniards join with Antonio. Willmore, Frederick and Blunt lay on like mad.

ANGELLICA.
Hold, I command you, if for me you fight!

WILLMORE
(*aside*). How heavenly fair she is! Ah, plague of her price!

ANGELLICA.
You sir, in buff, that first began this insolence –

WILLMORE.
'Tis true, I did so. I saw your charming picture and was wounded quite through my soul, and wanting a thousand crowns to procure my remedy, I assayed to lay this little picture to my bosom, which if you cannot allow me, I'll resign.

ANGELLICA.
No, you may take the trifle – if you can get it.

ANTONIO.
By heaven, you shall first ask us leave.

The bravos set upon Willmore and shoot at him. He dodges and disarms them.

Re-enter Belvile, Blunt, and Frederick.

BLUNT.
'Adsheartlikins, beat me a this sport and I'll ne'er wear sword more.

FREDERICK.
A plague on your dons; if they fight no better they'll ne'er recover Flanders.

BELVILE.
The devil's in thee for a mad fellow. Come, let's be gone whilst we're safe.

WILLMORE.
What the devil was't to them if she gave me the picture?

BLUNT.
'Adsheartlikins, 'tis ours by conquest. We'll pull it down.

ANGELLICA
(to Willmore). Stay, sir, and ere you all affront me farther let me know how you durst commit this outrage. To you I speak, sir, for you appear a gentleman.

WILLMORE.
To me, madam? –

ANGELLICA.
Come into the house. I would have words with thee.

WILLMORE.
Gentlemen; your servant.

BELVILE.
Is the devil in thee? Dost know the danger of ent'ring the house of an incensed courtesan?

ANGELLICA.
Fear not, sir, all I have to wound with is my eye. *(She goes in.)*

WILLMORE.
Death! Let me go!

BELVILE.
Yes, to your lodging if you will, but not in there.

FREDERICK.
Damn these gay harlots. Death, man, she'll murder thee!

WILLMORE.
Shall I not venture where a beauty calls?

BELVILE.
Pox, she'll as soon stab thee as lie with thee. You shall not go.

They draw.

FREDERICK.
Let him, colonel. We'll get as sound a whore for sixpence in the galley that's come in.

BLUNT.
'Adsheartlikins, I believe the gentlewoman means well.

BELVILE.
Well, take thy fortune, we'll expect you in the next street. Farewell, fool, farewell.

WILLMORE.
'Bye, colonel. *(Goes in.)*

FREDERICK.
The rogue's stark mad for a wench.

Exeunt.

Scene vii

A fine Chamber.
Enter Willmore, Angellica and Moretta.

MORETTA.
We shall never see good days again until all these fighting rogues are set to the galleys.

ANGELLICA.
Insolent sir, how durst you pull down my picture?

WILLMORE.
Rather, how durst you set it up to tempt poor am'rous mortals with so much excellence, which I find you have but too well consulted by the unmerciful price you set upon't? Is all this heaven of beauty shown to move despair in those that cannot buy?

ANGELLICA.
I sent for you to ask my pardon, sir, not to aggravate your crime. I thought I should have seen you at my feet imploring it.

WILLMORE.
You are deceived. I came to rail at you, and rail such truths too, as shall let you see the vanity of that pride which taught you how to set such price on sin, for such it is, for that which is love's due, is meanly bartered for.

ANGELLICA.
Alas, good captain, what pity 'tis your edifying doctrine will do no good upon me. Moretta, fetch the gentleman a glass, and let him survey himself to see what charms he has. – *(Aside, in a soft tone)* And guess my business.

MORETTA.
He knows himself of old: I believe those breeches and he have been acquainted ever since he was beaten at the battle of Worcester.

ANGELLICA.
Nay, do not abuse the poor creature.

MORETTA.
Good weatherbeaten swabber, will you set sail? The price is too high i'th' mouth for you, therefore tack off, I say.

WILLMORE.
Here, good forewoman of the shop, serve me and I'll be gone.

MORETTA.
Keep it to pay your laundress; your linen stinks of the gun room. Here's no selling by retail.

WILLMORE.
> Thou hast in thy time sold plenty of thy stale ware at a cheap rate.

MORETTA.
> Ay, the more silly kind heart I . . . You know the price . . .

WILLMORE.
> I grant you 'tis here set down, a thousand crowns a month. Pray, how much may come to my share for a pistole?

MORETTA.
> Abominable fellow, I tell thee we only sell by the whole piece.

WILLMORE.
> 'Tis very hard, the whole cargo or nothing. Faith, madam, my stock will not reach it. Yet I have countrymen in town, merchants of love like me; I'll see if they'll put in for a share. I am studying, madam, how to purchase you, though at present I am unprovided of money.

ANGELLICA
> (aside). Sure this from any other man would anger me; nor shall he know the conquest he has made.
> – Poor frambold man, how I despise this railing.

WILLMORE.
> Yes, I am poor and frambold. But I'm a gentleman,
> And one that scorns this baseness which you practise.
> Though poor – I would not sell myself to buy your person.
> Though I admire you strangely for your beauty,   .
> Yet I condemn your mercenary mind.

ANGELLICA.
> Why dost thou say I am mercenary?

MORETTA.
> Sirrah, fool! you must be gone.

ANGELLICA.
> How dare you take this freeedom. Withdraw!

MORETTA.
> Sure she's bewitched that stands thus tamely by
> And hears his saucy railings.

WILLMORE.   Withdraw!

Moretta withdraws.

ANGELLICA
> (to Willmore). Why dost thou say that I am mercenary.
> Suppose I saw you in the street and liked you,
> And came and knocked upon your captain's door
> And bade you bed me, would I wonder, sir,

If you asked me the price ere I enjoyed you?

WILLMORE.
> Why that's well said. And I'd enjoy you now
> At your own rate, but cannot. Thou see'st here
> The only sum I can command on earth:
> I know not where to eat when this is gone.
> Yet such a slave I am to love and beauty
> This last reserve I'll sacrifice to enjoy you.
> Nay, do not frown, I know you're to be bought,
> And, as I think, you would be bought by me.
> Nay, I will gaze, to let you see my strength.

Holds her, looks on her, and pauses and sighs.

> By heav'n, wench, I would not for the world
> Thy fame were half so fair as is thy face.

Turns her away from him.

ANGELLICA.
> If you have nothing else to say to me –

WILLMORE.
> Yes, you shall hear how infamous you are.

ANGELLICA.
> What, wilt thou moralise that hopes to buy me?
> You men are strangely partial to yourselves.
> What crime is mine that you would not now commit?
> Who made the laws by which you judge me? Men!
> And tell me, captain, are not men
> As mercenary as I?

WILLMORE.   Not I, I vow.

ANGELLICA.
> Nay, when some lady is proposed to you
> To be your wife, you do not ask how fair
> Or virtuous she is, but what's her fortune:
> Which, if but small, you cry 'She will not serve!'
> And basely leave her.

WILLMORE.   'Tis a barbarous custom.
> I scorn to defend it in our sex as I despise it
> In yours.

ANGELLICA.   Well said; why, now you speak more gently.
> Hast not enough good nature to forget
> My follies past? I blame thee not for thine,
> Although I nothing doubt they were as many.

WILLMORE.
> What's that to you or I that live i' the instant?

Then take my purse and me.

ANGELLICA.   Nay, not so fast.
Put up thy gold. I would not sell thee kindness
But for the sake of kindness.

WILLMORE. *(aside).*   What's her meaning?

ANGELLICA.
Thou shalt not buy my love.

WILLMORE. *(going).*   Why, then farewell.

ANGELLICA.
Nay, stay a little. Couldst thou not give me love?

WILLMORE.
I'faith, like anything.

ANGELLICA.   Confirm that faith,
And I'll –

WILLMORE.   Do what?

ANGELLICA.   – I cannot tell.
Perchance I'd . . . Nay I would not.
Tell me if you like me. Come,
Flatter me a little and 'twill please me.
Could'st not forget the merry but the mean effects
Of vanity which set me out for sale,
And as a lover prize my yielding joys.
Couldst not believe I might be wholly thine
Without considering I am mercenary?

WILLMORE.
I cannot tell, I must bethink me first.
(Aside) Ha! Death, methinks I'm going to believe her.
Curse on thy charming tongue! Dost thou return
My feigned contempt with so much subtlety?
Thou'st found the easiest way into my heart,
Although I know that all thou say'st is false.

ANGELLICA.
By all that's good, 'tis real. Now speak I open:
I never loved before though oft a mistress.
I fear you cannot credit my good faith.

WILLMORE.
Madam, I've been so often gulled and cheated,
That I've no faith left for the cozening sex,
Especially for women of your trade.

ANGELLICA.
'Tis well. This low esteem you have of me
May bring my heart to my command again:

For I have pride that yet surmounts my love.

She turns with pride; he holds her.

WILLMORE.
By heaven thou art brave and I admire thee strangely.
Throw off this pride, and show the power of love.
'Tis with those arms I can be only vanquished.

ANGELLICA.
I dare not hear thee talk; thou hast a charm
In every word that draws my heart away.
Thou hast undone me. Why art thou so soft?
Thy looks are hard and rough, and meant for war.
Couldst thou not storm on still? I then perhaps
Would be as free as thou and all as fiery.

WILLMORE.
(aside). Death, how she throws her flames about my soul!

ANGELLICA.
What, lingering still? Do I lack charms to please you?
Am I despised because enjoyed by others?
Are you so puritan a cavalier?
What, dost thou fear that I am over-used?
Try me: and you shall find the mine still golden.
Dost fear these lips are staled by ancient kisses,
Or that this body's paths are worn with use?
Nay, you shall find I am as fresh to reap
As any maid that has not found her harvest.

WILLMORE.
Take heed, fair creature, how you raise my hopes,
Which once fulfilled will give me all dominion:
There's not a joy thou hast in they hot store
I shall not then command.

ANGELLICA.   Content, I care not!

WILLMORE.
Then let's begin the account this happy minute!

ANGELLICA.
And will you pay me then the price I ask?

WILLMORE.
Oh! Why dost thou draw me from my holy worship
By showing me thou art not divinity?

ANGELLICA.
Nay, fool, the pay I mean's thy love for mine.
Can you give that?

WILLMORE.
Entirely.

ANGELLICA.
> Swear it then.

WILLMORE.
> Why, so I do. Then say no more, but in:
> Where I'll renew my vows and breathe 'em forth
> In such a wise thou shalt not doubt my ardour.

ANGELLICA.
> Thou hast a power too strong to be resisted.

> *Exeunt Willmore and Angellica.*

MORETTA.
> Is all our project fallen to this? To love such a shameroon; a very beggar; nay, a pirate beggar, whose business is to rifle and be gone; a no-purchase, no-pay tatterdemalion, and English picaroon: a rogue that fights for daily drink, and takes a pride in being loyally lousy? Oh, I could curse now, if I durst. This is the fate of most whores.
> Trophies, which from believing fops we win,
> Are spoils to those who cozen us again.

> *Exit*

Scene viii

The street.
Enter Florinda, Valeria, Hellena

VALERIA.
> Methinks we have learnt this trade of gypsies as readily as if we had been bred upon the road to Loretto. And yet I did so fumble when I told the stranger his fortune that I was afraid I should have told my own and yours by mistake. But methinks Hellena has been very serious ever since.

HELLENA.
> Hey, ho, I'm as sad as a lover's lute.

FLORINDA.
> I would give my garters she were in love, to be revenged upon her for abusing me.

VALERIA.
> How is't, Hellena?

HELLENA.
> Ah, would I had never seen my mad monsieur. And yet, for all your laughing, I am not in love. And yet this small acquaintance, o' my conscience, will never out of my head.

VALERIA.
> Ha! ha! ha! I laugh to think how thou art fitted with a lover, a fellow that I warrant loves every new face he sees.

HELLENA.
> Hum, he has not kept his word with me here, and may be taken up, elsewhere. That thought is not very pleasant to me. What the deuce should this be now that I feel?

VALERIA.
> What is't like?

HELLENA.
> Nay, the Lord knows, but if I should be hanged I cannot choose but be angry and afraid when I think that mad fellow should be in love with anybody but me. Would I could meet with some true damned gypsy, that I might know my fortune.

VALERIA.
> Know it! Why there's nothing so easy. Thou wilt love this wand'ring inconstant till thou find'st thyself hanged about his neck, and then be as mad to get free again.

FLORINDA.
> Yes, Valeria, we shall see her board his frigate and follow him over the ocean.

HELLENA.
> So, so, now you are both provided for there's no care taken of poor me.

VALERIA.
> How? I provided for?

HELLENA.
> Thou did'st so flaunt and ogle that I thought you meant to lure all the city to thy bed.

VALERIA.
> Nay, my man was coy.

HELLENA.
> Well, and if you are not yet a lover, 'tis an art soon learnt – that I find. (*Sighs.*)

FLORINDA.
> I wonder how you learnt to love so easily. I had a thousand charms to meet my eyes and ears ere I could yield, and 'twas the knowledge of Belvile's merit took my soul. Thou art too rash, to give a heart at first sigh.

HELLENA.
> Hang your considering lover! I never thought beyond the fancy that 'twas a very pretty, idle, silly kind of pleasure to pass one's

time with. To write little soft nonsensical billets, and with great difficulty and danger receive answers in which I shall have my beauty praised, my wit admired, though little or none, and have the vanity and power to know I am desirable. But now I have the more inclination to be rash, because I am to be a nun, and so shall not be suspected to have any such earthly thoughts about me, but when I walk thus – and sigh thus – they'll think my mind's upon my nunnery and cry, 'How happy 'tis she's so resolved.' But not a word of man.

FLORINDA.
What a mad creature's this!

VALERIA.
See, here come our lovers back. Let's plague them still.

HELLENA.
But where's my inconstant? Let's step aside, and we may learn something.

They go aside.

Scene ix

The same.
Enter Belvile, Frederick and Blunt.

BELVILE.
What means this! The picture's taken in.

BLUNT.
It may be the wench is good natured, and will be kind gratis.

BELVILE.
I rather think she has cut his throat and is fled. Let's knock and ask for him.

HELLENA.
My heart goes a-pit, a-pat, for fear 'tis my man they talk of.

ALL CRY.
Willmore.

Enter Biskey and Moretta above.

BISKEY.
What would you have?

BELVILE.
Tell the stranger that entered here about two hours ago that his friends stay here for him.

MORETTA.
A curse upon him from Moretta.
He's coming to you.

She goes. Enter Willmore below.

HELLENA.
Ay, ay 'tis he. Oh, how this vexes me!

BELVILE.
And how and how, dear lad, has fortune smiled? Are we to raise up altars to her, or break her windows, hah?

WILLMORE.
Does not my fortune sit triumphant on my brow? Dost not see the little wanton god there all gay and smiling? Have I not an air about my face and eyes that distinguish me from the crowd of common lovers. Oh, such a bona roba! To sleep in her arms is lying in fresco, all perfumed air about me.

HELLENA
(*aside*). Here's fine encouragement for me to fool on!

WILLMORE.
Hark'ee, where didst thou purchase that rich Canary we drank today? The juice was divine.

BELVILE.
Well, here, take a bottle and let's hear the story of your success.

FREDERICK.
Would not French wine do better?

WILLMORE.
Damn the hungry balderdash! Cheerful sack has a generous virtue in't, inspiring a successful confidence, gives eloquence to the tongue and vigour to the soul, and has in a few hours completed all my hopes and wishes! There's nothing left to raise a new desire in me . . . And, gentlemen, study, study to what you want for here are friends that will supply us. (*Jingles gold.*) Hark what a charming sound they make . . .

BLUNT.
But hark'ee, sir, you are not married, are you?

WILLMORE.
All the honey of matrimony but none of the sting, friend.

BLUNT.
Pox on't, thou'rt a fortunate rogue.

BLUNT.
'Adsheartlikins, here's two of us provided for!

FREDERICK.
By this light, y'are happy men. Oh, for my little gypsy now.

BLUNT.

Fortune is pleased to smile on us, gentlemen, to smile on us.

Enter Sancho; the cavaliers go aside.

SANCHO.

Sir, my lady expects you. She has removed all that might oppose your will and pleasure, and is impatient till you come.

BLUNT.

I'll attend you, sir – Oh the happiest rogue! Her husband is gone hence. I'll take no leave, lest they either dog me or stay me.

Exit with Sancho.

FREDERICK.

Lo, how Ned's in a lure. I hope she'll dress him for our mirth, cheat him of all, then have him well-favouredly banged, and turned out at midnight.

BELVILE.

So, captain, the little gypsy is forgot?

WILLMORE.

A mischief on thee for putting her into my thoughts! I had quite forgot her else, and this night's debauch had drunk her quite down.

Florinda, Valeria and Hellena approach.

HELLENA.

Had it so, good captain!

WILLMORE

(*aside*). Ha! I hope she did not hear me!

FREDERICK.

Ha! Our gypsies! To 'em Colonel.

HELLENA.

What, afraid of such a champion?

WILLMORE.

Oh, you're a fine lady of your word, are you not? To make a man languish a whole day –

HELLENA.

In tedious search of me.

WILLMORE.

Egad, child thou'rt in the right. Hadst thou seen what a melancholy dog I have been since I last saw you – faith sweetheart, thou wouldst pity me.

HELLENA

(*aside*). Now if I should be hanged I can't be angry with him, he dissembles so heartily – Alas, good captain, what pains you have taken; now were I a beast not to reward so true a servant.

WILLMORE.

Poor soul, that's kindly said; I see thou barest a conscience. Come then, for a beginning, show me thy dear face.

HELLENA.

I'm afraid, my small acquaintance, you have been staying that swingeing stomach you boasted of this morning. I then remember my little collation would have gone down with you without the sauce of a handsome face. Is your stomach so queasy now?

WILLMORE.

Faith, long fasting, child, spoils a man's appetite. Yet if you durst treat, I could so lay about me still –

VALERIA.

And would you fall to before a priest says grace?

WILLMORE.

Oh fie, fie, what an old out-of-fashioned thing hast thou named? Thou couldst not dash me more out of countenance shouldst thou show me an ugly face.

Whilst he is seemingly courting Hellena, enter Angellica, Moretta, Biskey, and Sebastian all in masquerade. Angellica sees Willmore and stares.

ANGELLICA.

Heavens, 'tis he! And passionately fond to see another woman!

HELLENA.

You see, captain, how willing I am to be friends with you, till time and ill luck make us lovers; and ask you the question first rather than put your modesty to the blush by asking me. For alas, I know you captains are such strict men, and such severe observers of your vows to chastity, that 'twill be hard to prevail with your tender conscience to marry a young willing maid.

WILLMORE.

Do not abuse me, for fear I should take thee at thy word and marry thee indeed, which I'm sure would be revenge sufficient.

HELLENA.

O' my conscience, that would be our destiny because we are both of one humour. I am as inconstant as you. For I have considered, captain, that a handsome woman has a great deal to do whilst her face is good, for then is our harvest-time to gather friends. And should I in these days of my youth catch a fit or foolish constancy, I were undone; 'tis loitering by daylight in our great journey. Therefore, I declare I'll allow but one year for love, one year for indifference, and one year for hate, and then go hang yourself, for I profess myself the gay, the kind, and the inconstant. The devil's in't if this won't please you!

WILLMORE.
Oh, most damnably. I have a heart with a hole quite through it too; no prison mine, to keep a mistress in.

ANGELLICA
(aside). Perjured man! How I believe thee now!

HELLENA.
Well, I see our business as well as humours are alike, yours to cozen as many maids as will trust you, and I as many men as I have faith. See if I have not as desperate a lying lover's look as you can have for the heart of you. (Pulls off her vizard; he starts.) How do you like it, captain?

WILLMORE.
Like it! By heaven, I never saw so much beauty! Oh, the charms of those sprightly blue eyes! That strangely fair face, full of smiles and dimples! Those soft round melting cherry lips and small even white teeth! Not to be expressed, but silently adored!

ANGELLICA.
I can endure no more, for if I do my jealousy will destroy my reason. Sebastian, follow that woman and learn who 'tis.

Exit into above.

WILLMORE.
Oh, one look more and strike me dumb.

This while Florinda is talking to Belvile, who stands sullenly; Frederick courting Valeria.

FLORINDA.
Nay, stay sir. (To Valeria.) What shall I do next?

VALERIA
(to Belvile). Prithee, dear stranger, though you have not yet your love Florinda, you see my friend frankly offers you hers to play with in the meantime.

BELVILE.
Faith, madam, I am sorry I can't play at her game.

FREDERICK
(to Valeria). Pray leave your intercession and mind your own affair. They'll better agree apart. He's a modest sigher in company, but alone no woman 'scapes him.

FLORINDA.
Sure he does but rally. Yet, if it should be true, I'll tempt him farther. (To Belvile.) Believe me, noble stranger, I'm no common mistress. And for a little proof on't, wear this jewel. Nay, take it, sir.

BELVILE.
Madam, why am I chose out of all mankind to be the object of your bounty?

VALERIA.
There's another civil question asked.

FREDERICK
(aside). Pox of's modesty; it spoils his own markets and hinders mine.

FLORINDA.
Sir, from my window I have often seen you, and women of my quality have so few opportunities for love that we ought to lose none.

FREDERICK
(to Valeria). Here's a woman! When shall I be blest with so much kindness from your fair mouth?

VALERIA.
When my sister thrives.

FREDERICK
(aside to Belvile). Take the jewel, fool!

BELVILE.
You tempt me strangely, madam, every way – And but for a vow I've made to a very fair lady, this goodness had subdued me.

FREDERICK
(aside to Belvile). Pox on't, be kind, in pity to me be kind. For I am to thrive but as you treat her friend. Belvile!

They retire.

FLORINDA.
So he's true to his Florinda.

VALERIA.
'Tis well, let's after them.

HELLENA.
Then tell me what you did in yonder house and I'll unmask.

WILLMORE.
Yonder house?

HELLENA.

Yonder house.

WILLMORE.

Yonder house. Oh, I went to . . . why, there's a friend of mine lives there.

HELLENA.

What, a she or a he friend?

WILLMORE.

A man, upon my honour, a man.

HELLENA.

Methinks I see the little wanton god on thy brow all gay and smiling. 'Ah, such a bona roba!' Was this your man friend too? 'To be in her arms is lying in fresco, all perfumed air about me.'

WILLMORE.

Well, well, madam, then you can see there are ladies in the world that will not be cruel. There are, madam, there are.

HELLENA.

And there be men, too, as fine, wild, inconstant, fellows as yourself. There be, captain, there be. Therefore, I'm resolved –

WILLMORE.

Oh!

HELLENA.

To see your face no more –

WILLMORE.

Oh!

HELLENA.

Till tomorrow.

WILLMORE.

Egad, you frighted me.

HELLENA.

Nor then neither, unless you'll swear never to see that lady more.

WILLMORE.

See her! Why, never to think of womankind again.

HELLENA.

Kneel, and swear.

He kneels, she gives him her hand.

WILLMORE.

I do, never to think, to see, to love, nor lie, with any but thyself.

HELLENA.

Kiss the book.

WILLMORE.

Oh, most religiously. (*Kisses her hand.*)

HELLENA

(*aside*). Now what a wicked creature am I, to damn a proper fellow.

VALERIA

(*to Florinda*). Come sister, we must stay no longer. 'Tis e'en dark.

FLORINDA

(*to Belvile*). I'll leave this with you, sir, that when I'm gone you may repent the opportunity you have lost by your modesty.

Gives him the jewel, which is her picture, and exit. He gazes after her.

WILLMORE

(*to Hellena*). 'Twill be an age till tomorrow, and till then I will most impatiently expect you. Adieu, my dear pretty angel.

Exeunt all the women.

BELVILE.

Ha! Florinda's picture! 'Twas she herself. What a dull dog was I!

FREDERICK.

This comes of your modesty. A pox o' your vow.

BELVILE.

Willmore, the blessed'st opportunity lost!

WILLMORE.

Ah, rogue! Such eyes! Such a face! Such a mouth! Such teeth! And so much wit!

BELVILE.

All, all, and a thousand charms besides.

WILLMORE.

Why, dost thou know her?

BELVILE.

Know her! Ay, ay, and a pox take me with all my heart for being so modest.

WILLMORE.

But hark'ee, friend of mine, are you my rival?

BELVILE.

I understand thee not. I'm mad! (*Shows the picture.*)

FREDERICK.
See here.

WILLMORE.
Ha! Whose picture's this? 'Tis a fine wench!

FREDERICK.
The colonel's mistress, sir.

WILLMORE.
Oh, oh, here. (*Gives the picture back*.) I thought't had been another prize. Come, come, another bottle will set thee right again.

BELVILE.
I am confident to try, and by that time 'twill be late enough for our design in Florinda's garden.

FREDERICK.
Agreed.

WILLMORE.
Love does all day the soul's great empire keep,
But wine at night lulls the soft god asleep.

Exeunt singing.

Scene x

A chamber.
Enter Lucetta, finely dressed, and Sancho.

SANCHO.
Haste, haste, he'll be here straight.

LUCETTA.
Go I not gorgeous thus?

SANCHO.
Now you look finely.

LUCETTA.
I would I were in truth as fine as now I seem to be. Pray Sancho, let me bear myself gently with my Englishman a little ere we flea him.

SANCHO.
Fie, how thou dream'st, Lucetta. Are not thy shoulders as laced as mine with galley lashes? Wear not thy dress so low lest he spy them.

LUCETTA.
Nay, 'tis good to go thus when 'tis Carnival.

SANCHO.
Well, thou shalt bear yourself gently enough to make him hot, but not so hot that he undo you. I'll thump you if you lick him.

LUCETTA.
Nay, fear me not.

BLUNT.
Yoo-hoo-hoo!

SANCHO.
He comes.

Enter Blunt.

BLUNT.
Lady, I must beg your pardon for coming this late. There was an accident stayed me beyond my expectation.

LUCETTA
(*Very demure*). Sir, you are not only master of thy own, but of my time as well. I dare not say how much your absence has afflicted me, but rather what joy your presence brings these eyes that love and adore her friend.

BLUNT.
I – you . . . (*Aside*) Pox on't, that I had but some fine things to say to her, such as lovers use. 'Adsheartlikins, sweet soul, I am not used to compliment, but I'm an honest gentleman, and thy humble servant. (*Aside*) I was a fool not to learn of Fred a little by heart before I came . . .

LUCETTA.
You are sad, sir. All's well. My old jealous husband is gone hence, so fear you not but come a little nearer. Your eyes are blue – do you love me? Nay, say so, though you do not. Nay, but be tender. For I am so delicate a lady that I am ashamed to tell how my heart aches for you.

BLUNT.
Gentle soul, why dost thou blush and hide thy head? I never had but one heart, a plain one and as honest, and that's thine.

LUCETTA.
Faith, thy sweet face and shape have made me your absolute captive.

BLUNT.
(*aside*). Kind heart, how prettily she talks! Egad, I'll show her husband a Spanish trick. I'll send him out of the world and marry her; she's damnably in love with me.

She weeps.

Why dost weep? Come, no tears. You should smile on love.

Come, let's retire, 'tis late and love would roost.

LUCETTA.

Will you be gentle?

BLUNT.

Ay, I'll but sip thee as a cat licks cream. Yet 'adsheartlikins, I ache for thee.

LUCETTA.

Ah, sir, you speak my pains also. And my desires and love exceed your wishes, though I blush to say so.

BLUNT.

'Tis well, we both are hot.

LUCETTA.

Let's to bed and assay who is the hotter.
I'll go in and undress me, and be with you instantly.

She goes. He undresses.

BLUNT.

'Tis a rare girl, and this one night's enjoyment with her will be worth all the days I ever passed in Essex. Sure, her embraces will far excel all the pleasures I have ever tasted; for I ne'er loved, nor was beloved till now. This is Love's holy-day; the rest were working days, in which I but ploughed the sex. Our dull cold kisses were common seed, thoughtless sown and full of weed, not of force to kindle a heart. Here every look or touch inflames or burns my blood. 'Tis pleasure thus to be stung; I'll take her home with me into England.

Re-enter Lucetta, undressed, with a candle.

LUCETTA.

Are you not undressed yet?

BLUNT.

As much as my impatience will permit.

LUCETTA.

Hold, sir, put out the light; it may betray us else.

BLUNT.

Anything; I need no other light but that of thine eyes –
(*Aside*) 'Adsheartlikins, there I think I had it.

Puts out the candle, and takes off the rest of his garments. He gropes about to find her.

Where are you, sweetest?

SANCHO.

A pretty love-trick this. (*Hits Blunt.*)

BLUNT.

Ha! (*He is thrown down a trap.*)

SANCHO.

Ha! Ha! Ha! He's dispatched finely.

LUCETTA.

Now, sir, had I been coy, we had missed of this booty.

SANCHO.

Nay, when I saw 'twas a subtantial fool, I was mollified. But when you seem to dote upon a seranading coxcomb, it makes me rage.

LUCETTA.

You know I was never guilty of that folly, my dear Sancho, but with yourself.

SANCHO.

But come, let's see what we have got by this. A rich coat; sword; these breeches, too, are well lined!

LUCETTA.

See here, a gold watch!

SANCHO.

A purse – Ha! Gold! At least two hundred pistoles!

LUCETTA.

A bunch of diamond rings, and one with the family arms! A gold box, with a medal of his king, and his lady mother's picture!

SANCHO.

See, the waistband of his breeches have a mine of gold – old queen Bess's! We have a quarrel to her ever since eighty-eight.

LUCETTA.

See, a bracelet of bowed gold! . . . Yet, for all this, I fear his being a stranger may make a noise and hinder our trade with them hereafter.

SANCHO.

That's our security; he is not only a stranger to us, but to the country too. The common sewer into which he is descended conducts him into another street. He knows neither your name, nor that of the street where your house is; nay, nor the way to his own lodgings.

LUCETTA.

And art thou not an unmerciful rogue, not to afford him one night for all this?

SANCHO.

Blame me not, Lucetta, to keep as much of thee as I can to

myself. Come, that thought makes me wanton; let's to bed. I'll
lock up these. (*Aside.*)
This is the fleece which fools do bear,
Designed for witty men to shear.

He goes.

LUCETTA.
This gold will buy us things. But what shall I do next tomorrow.
Alas, I curse my future that has made me a slave to Sancho,
since I was sold. Would I had coin enough to fly to England and
try my fortune as the colonel did. But what base means we girls
o' the galleys must submit to, ere we can gain our ends. A
common whore, oh fie: one that must yield to all beastly
embraces, yea, all the nasty devices men's lust can invent; nay,
not only obey but blow the fire too, and hazard all diseases when
their lust commands. And so sometimes we are enjoyed afore-
times, but never after.

Blunt calls out below.

And yet I cannot but laugh at this English fool. If I cannot rise
in this bad world, yet 'tis some recompense to bring such a
fellow down. Lo, now is this bull calf as naked as I was once on
shipboard, and now I pity him. There's for thee, poor Essex
calf. (*She throws her drawers down into the hole where Blunt has
fallen. Sancho calls her outside.*)

I come, I come.

*She goes. Blunt climbs out of the common sewer, all dirty and
beaten, with nothing on but the thing of Lucetta's which she threw
down.*

BLUNT
(*climbing up*). Oh, Lord, I've got out at last. Alas, I know not
where I am now, nor how to get me home. Oh, what a dog was I!
'Tis plain, fool was writ upon my forehead!

Music without.

Hark!
These rogues and masquers must not see me thus.
I fear some beastly ballad to my sorrow
Will be devised and sung here on the morrow;
And yet I know there's many here among
Would in my place, have been in likewise stung;
And though you've better arts to hide your follies,
'Adsheartlikins, you're all as errant cullies!

Masquers come in and mock him and pursue him.

INTERVAL

Scene xi

Night. A garden.
Enter Florinda in an undress.

FLORINDA.
Now am I in my way to happiness, and now I ache for Belvile. I
have got myself free from Callis, my brother thinks not of me,
and I have by good fortune got the key of the garden back door
and which I have unlocked to prevent my Belvile's knocking.
Yet a little noise will now alarm my brother. I am as fearful as a
young thief, and as joyful as – Hark! What noise is that? Oh,
'twas the wind that played amongst the boughs. Belvile stays
long, methinks, it's time. O fie, the wind has ruffled my hair.
I'll get a mirror to make it fine again.

She gets one. Enter Wilmore, drunk.

WILLMORE.
What the devil is become of these fellows Belvile and
Frederick? They promised to stay at the next corner for me.
Now, whereabouts am I? A garden! A very convenient place to
sleep in. Ha! What has God sent us here? A female! By this
light, a woman! I'm a dog if it be not a very wench!

FLORINDA.
He's come! Ha! Who's there?

WILLMORE.
Sweet soul, let me salute thy shoestring.

FLORINDA
(*aside*). 'Tis not my Belvile – Who are you, and from whence
come you?

WILLMORE.
Prithee, prithee, child, not so many hard questions! Let it
suffice I am here, child. Come, come kiss me.

FLORINDA.
Good gods! What luck is mine!

WILLMORE.
Only good luck, child, parlous good luck. 'Tis a delicate
shining wench. By this hand, she's perfumed, and smells like
any nosegay. Prithee, dear soul, let's not play the fool and lose
time, precious time. For as God shall save me, I'm as honest a
fellow as breathes, though I'm a little disguised at present.
Come, I say, Why, thou mayst be free with me. I'll be very
secret . . .

FLORINDA.
Heavens! What a filthy beast is this!

WILLMORE.

I am so, and thou ought'st the sooner to lie with me for that reason. For look you, child, there will be no sin in't, because 'twas neither designed nor premeditated; 'tis pure accident on both sides. Come be kind without any more idle prating.

FLORINDA.

Oh, I am ruined! Wicked man, unhand me!

WILLMORE.

Wicked? Egad, child, those eyes of thine gave the first blow, the first provocation. So doth thy habit. Come, prithee let's lose no time, I say. This is a fine convenient place.

FLORINDA.

If you do not instantly let me go I'll cry murder, rape, or anything.

WILLMORE.

A rape! Come, come, you lie, you baggage, you lie. Why at this time of night was your cobweb door set open, dear spider, but to catch flies?

FLORINDA.

Sir, can you think –

WILLMORE.

That you would do't for nothing? Oh, oh, I find what you would be at. Look here, here's a pistole for you.

FLORINDA.

For heaven's sake, sir, as you're a gentleman –

WILLMORE.

So now, now, she would be wheedling me for more! What, you will not take it then? Come, come, take it or I'll put it up again, for look ye, I never give more. Come, no struggling to be gone. But an y'are good at a dumb wrestle, I'm for ye. (*She struggles with him.*)

Enter Belvile and Frederick.

BELVILE.

A pox of this mad rogue! I'm angry that we've lost him.

FREDERICK.

But you were so hasty, colonel, to be gone.

FLORINDA.

Help! Murder! Help! Oh, I am ruined!

BELVILE.

Ha! Sure that's Florinda's voice! (*Comes up to them.*) Villain, let go that lady!

FLORINDA.

Belvile!

BELVILE.

Willmore!

FLORINDA.

Heavens! My brother too is coming, and 'twill be impossible to escape. Belvile, walk under my chamber window, from whence I'll give you some instructions what to do. This rude man has undone us.

Exit.

Enter Pedro and Stephano and other servants with lights.

PEDRO.

I'm betrayed! Run, Stephano, and see if Florinda be safe.

Exit Stephano.

– So, whoe'er they be, all is not well. I'll to Florinda's chamber.

Going out, meets Stephano.

STEPHANO.

You need not, sir, the poor lady's fast asleep, and thinks no harm. I would not awake her, sir, for fear of frightening her with your danger.

PEDRO.

Rascals, how came the garden door open?

STEPHANO.

That question comes too late, sir. Some of my fellow servants masquerading, I'll warrant.

PEDRO.

Masquerading! A lewd custom to debauch our youth! There's something more in this than I imagine.

Exeunt.

Scene xii

The street.
Enter Belvile in rage, Frederick holding him, Willmore melancholy.

WILLMORE.

Why, how the devil should I know Florinda?

BELVILE.

Ah, plague of your ignorance! If it had not been Florinda, must you be a beast? A brute? A senseless swine?

WILLMORE.
Well, sir, you see I am endued with patience. I can bear.
Though egad, y'are very free with me, methinks.

BELVILE.
Peace, brute, whilst thou'rt safe.

WILLMORE.
Nay, nay, I'm an unlucky dog, that's certain.

BELVILE.
Ah, curse upon the star that ruled my birth, or whatsoever
other influence that makes me still so wretched.

WILLMORE.
Thou break'st my heart with these complaints. There is no star
in fault, no influence but sack, the cursed sack I drunk.

FREDERICK.
Why, how the devil came you so drunk?

WILLMORE.
Why, how the devil came you so sober?

FREDERICK.
Prithee, dear colonel, forgive him. He's sorry for his fault.

BELVILE.
He's always so after he has done a mischief.

WILLMORE.
By this light, I took her for an errant harlot.

BELVILE.
Damn your debauched opinion! Tell me, sot, hadst thou so
much sense and light about thee to distinguish her woman, and
couldst not see something about her face and person to strike an
awful reverence into thy soul?

WILLMORE.
Faith no, I considered her as mere a woman as I could wish.

BELVILE.
'Sdeath, I have no patience. Draw, or I'll kill you!

WILLMORE.
Let that alone till tomorrow, and if I set not all right again, use
your pleasure.

BELVILE.
Damn it, tomorrow she's Antonio's.
Would I could meet once with my happy rival.

WILLMORE.
What then?

BELVILE.
Let thy own reason, or my rage, instruct thee.

WILLMORE.
Show me the man and I'll do his business.

BELVILE.
I know him no more than thou, or if I did I should not need thy
aid.
I'll plant myself under Florinda's window
And if I find no comfort there, I'll die.

Exeunt Belvile and Frederick.
Enter Sebastian and Biskey.

WILLMORE.
Why, this is Angellica's house, I promised the kind baggage to
lie with her tonight.

Offers to go in. Enter Antonio.

ANTONIO.
Hast thou received the thousand crowns I sent?

BISKEY.
Yea, 'tis with the old woman within.

SEBASTIAN.
You're welcome, sir.

WILLMORE.
Who the devil have we here?

Enter Moretta above.

MORETTA.
Don Antonio?

ANTONIO.
Yea, and come to claim the prize I paid for.

WILLMORE.
How is this? A picaroon going to board my frigate? – Here's one
chase gun for you!

Drawing his sword, jostles Antonio, who is wounded.

SEBASTIAN.
The mad Englishman has set upon my lord again. Kill him!

MORETTA.
The mad fellow's back. We're all undone!

DIEGO.
Ring the alarm bell!

FREDERICK.

The mad rogue's in at it again.

Alarm bell. Belvile and Frederick return at noise of fighting.

MORETTA.

Ha! Help! A man killed!

WILLMORE.

How, killed? Then I'll go home to sleep.

Frederick carries him out.

BELVILE.

Killed? Who should it be? Pray heaven the rogue is safe, for all my quarrel to him.

ANTONIO.

I'm wounded.

Belvile comes to aid him. Antonio swings his sword.

Ah!

Enter from all sides Diego and Soldiers with guns.

ANTONIO.

Secure the villain.

BELVILE.

Do not mistake my charity for villainy. I came to his assistance.

ANTONIO.

This Englishman has set up me twice.

BELVILE.

Not I.

ANTONIO

(*to Diego*). Carry him to my apartment till you have farther orders from me.

BELVILE.

Has my humanity made me a criminal?

ANTONIO.

Look well to the villain there.

Antonio exits.
Soldiers knock out Belvile and exit.

DIEGO.

St. Jago! Swords drawn in the Carnival time!

He goes.

Scene xiii

A fine room, dark.
Enter Soldiers with Belvile, and throw him down.

BELVILE.

What a cursed chance is this! When shall I be weary of railing on fortune, who is resolved never to turn with smiles upon me? Two such defeats in one night. I am here a prisoner. But where, heaven knows . . . Yet this is nothing to the torture my soul bows with when I think of losing my fair, my dear Florinda. Hark, a door opens. A light! Now shall I die like a dog, without defence.

Enter Antonio in undress, with a light, his arm in a scarf, and a sword under his arm. Diego with him.

ANTONIO.

Sir, I come to know what injuries I have done you English, that could provoke you to so mean an action as to attack me basely without allowing time for my defence? 'Tis the Viceroy's son whom you have wounded.

BELVILE.

The Viceroy's son! (*Aside*) Death and confusion! Don Antonio, the man of all the world I would destroy! Sir, for a man in my circumstances to plead innocence would look like fear. But view me well, and you will find no marks of coward on me, nor anything that betrays that brutality you accuse me with.

ANTONIO.

In vain sir, you impose upon my sense. You are not only he who drew on me tonight, but yesterday before the same house, that of Angellica.

BELVILE.

If you will kill me, I cannot fear you'll do it basely.

ANTONIO.

No sir, I'll make you fit for a defence with this.

Gives him the sword.

BELVILE.

This gallantry surprises me, nor know I how to use this present, sir, against a man so brave.

ANTONIO.

You shall not need. For know, I come to snatch you from a danger that is decreed against you by our laws of Carnival: perhaps your life, or long imprisonment.

BELVILE

How shall I pay this generosity (*Aside*) Death! Obliged by him who would wed Florinda.

ANTONIO.
>You seem disordered, sir.

BELVILE.
>Yes, trust me, I am, and 'tis with pain that a man receives such bounties who wants the power to pay 'em back again.

ANTONIO.
>To gallant spirits 'tis indeed uneasy, but you may quickly overpay me, sir.

BELVILE.
>Oh, I'm impatient, sir, to be discounting the mighty debt I owe you. Command me quickly.

ANTONIO.
>I have a quarrel with a rival, sir, about a woman whom we love.

BELVILE
>(*aside*). Death. 'Tis Florinda he means!

ANTONIO.
>My rival challenged me yesterday to meet him on the Molo as soon as day appeared.

BELVILE
>(*aside*). Death, who should this be?

ANTONIO.
>But tonight's quarrel has made my arm unfit to guide a sword.

BELVILE.
>I apprehend you, sir. You'd have me kill the man that lays a claim to the maid you speak of. I'll do't. I'll fly to do't!

ANTONIO.
>Sir, I shall rob you of the glory on't, for you must fight under my name and dress.

BELVILE.
>That opinion must be strangely obliging that makes you think I can personate the brave Antonio . . .

ANTONIO.
>You say too much to my advantage. Come, sir, the day appears that calls you forth. Put on this habit.

>*Diego gives Belvile his carnival gear, and exits with Antonio.*

BELVILE
>(*dressing*). Fantastic fortune, thou deceitful light,
>That cheats the wearied traveller by night,
>Though on a precipice each step you tread,
>I am resolved to follow where you lead.

>*Exit.*

Scene xiv

A street.
Enter Florinda, hooded, with Stephano.

FLORINDA
>(*aside*). I'm dying with my fears. Belvile's not coming to my window last night as I bade him makes me believe that all those fears are true. Stephano, canst thou not tell with whom my brother is to fight?

STEPHANO.
>No, madam, they were both in masquerade. I was by when they challenged one another yesterday, and they had decided the quarrel then, but were prevented by some cavaliers, which made 'em put it off till now. But I am sure 'tis about you that your brother fights.

FLORINDA
>(*aside*). Nay, then, 'tis with Belvile, for what other lover have I that dares fight for me except Antonio, and he is too much in favour with my brother ever to fight with him . . .

STEPHANO.
>Madam, your brother's coming. If my master sees me, I shall be hanged for being your conductor. I escaped narrowly for the excuse I made for you last night i'th'garden.

FLORINDA.
>And I'll reward thee.

>*Exit Stephano.*
>*Enter Don Pedro in his masking habit.*

PEDRO.
>Antonio's late today. The place will fill, and we may be prevented. (*Walks about.*)

FLORINDA
>(*aside*). Antonio? Sure, I heard amiss.

PEDRO.
>But who will not excuse a happy lover
>When soft fair arms confine the yielding neck?
>I fear he's been with fair Angellica.

>*Enter Belvile dressed in Antonio's clothes.*

BELVILE.
>This must be he.

PEDRO.
>Antonio! Good morrow.

FLORINDA
>(*aside*). 'Tis not Belvile; half my fears are vanished.

BELVILE.
You're early, sir. I do not use to be outdone this way.

PEDRO.
The wretched, sir, are watchful, and 'tis enough you've the advantage of me in Angellica.

BELVILE
(*aside*). Angellica! Have I mistook my man? Or has Antonio?

PEDRO.
Come, sir, you know our terms.

BELVILE.
No talking. I am ready, sir.

Offers to fight, Florinda runs in.

FLORINDA
(*to Belvile*). Oh, hold! Whoe'er you be. If you strike here, I die!

PEDRO.
Florinda!

BELVILE
(*aside*). Florinda imploring for my rival!

PEDRO.
Away, this kindness is unseasonable.

Puts her by. They fight. She runs in just as Belvile disarms Pedro.

FLORINDA.
By all you hold most dear, by her you love,
Beseech you, touch him not.

BELVILE.
By her I love?
See, I obey, and here resign
The useless trophy of my victory.

Lays his sword at her feet.

PEDRO.
Well, Antonio, 'tis well. You've done enough to prove you love Florinda.

BELVILE.
Love Florinda! Love her? Here, sir, your sword again.

Snatches up the sword and gives it to him.

Upon this truth I'll fight my life away.

PEDRO.
No, you've redeemed my friendship, and my sister.

He pulls off his vizard to show his face.

BELVILE.
Don Pedro!

PEDRO.
Antonio, can you resign your claims to Angellica, and give your heart entirely to Florinda?

BELVILE.
Entire! This minute let me make her mine:
I can delay my happiness no longer.

PEDRO.
This minute let it be: no time so proper.
This night my father will arrive from Rome
And possibly may hinder what we purpose.

FLORINDA
(*aside*). Oh, heavens! This minute? I am quite undone.

PEDRO.
That we may not be observed, do you walk off to St. Peter's church, where I will meet you and conclude your happiness.

BELVILE.
I'll meet you there.

PEDRO.
I'll fetch a father.

FLORINDA.
Stay, sir, I have not yet prepared my heart
To entertain so strange a guest.

PEDRO.
Away; this modesty's assumed too late.

BELVILE.
Oh heaven, madam, know you what you do?

FLORINDA.
Do? Despise the man that lays a tyrant's claim
To what he ought to conquer by submission.

BELVILE.
You do not know me. Move this way a little.
(*To Pedro.*)
She's coy. 'Tis best I speak to her in private.
(*Draws her aside.*)

PEDRO.
I'll be with you straight.

FLORINDA.
Sir, you may force me even to the altar,
But you shall never force me to be thine.

BELVILE.
Oh, do not lose so blest an opportunity!

Pulls off his vizard.

See, 'tis your Belvile, not Antonio.

FLORINDA.
Belvile!

BELVILE.
At last we're met in our own person, sweet.
Then fear you not, if we but use our wit,
Doubt not that we shall win our long-fought joys.

FLORINDA.
How long have I waited for this happy minute.

As they are talking, enter Willmore, finely dressed.

WILLMORE.
Ah, Belvile! Good morrow noble colonel.

Runs and embraces him.

PEDRO.
Belvile!

BELVILE.
Hell and confusion seize thee!

PEDRO.
Ha! I beg your pardon, sir.

Takes Florinda from him.

BELVILE.
Nay, touch her not. She's mine by conquest, sir.
I won her by my sword.

WILLMORE.   Faith, didst thou so?
Then, child, egad, we'll keep her by the sword.

Draws on Pedro and attacks him. Belvile goes between.

BELVILE.
Stand off!
Thou'rt so profanely lewd, so curst by heaven,
All quarrels thou espousest must be fatal.

WILLMORE.
Nay, an you be so hot, my valour's coy.
And shall be courted when you want it next.

Puts up his sword.

BELVILE.
(*to Pedro*). You know I ought to claim a victor's right,

But you're the brother to divine Florinda;
I durst not hurt the man she holds so dear.

PEDRO.
'Twas by Antonio's, not by Belvile's sword
This question should have been decided, sir.
I must confess much to your bravery's due,
But I am nicely punctual in my word,
And this mistake another time shall clear.
(*Aside to Florinda as they are going out.*)
This was some plot between you and Belvile,
But I'll prevent you. Sister, come away.

Pedro takes Florinda out.

Belvile looks after her and begins to walk up and down in rage.

WILLMORE.
Do not be modest now and lose the woman. But if we shall fetch
her back so –

BELVILE.
Do not speak to me!

WILLMORE.
I know I've done some mischief, but I'm so dull a puppy that
I'm the son of a whore if I know how or where. Prithee inform
my understanding.

BELVILE.
Leave me, I say, and leave me instantly!

WILLMORE.
I will not leave you in this humour, nor till I know my crime.

BELVILE.
Death, I'll tell you, sir –

Draws and runs at Willmore; who runs out, Belvile after him.
Enter Frederick, Angellica, Moretta, and Sebastian.

ANGELLICA.
Ha! Sebastian, is that not Willmore? Haste! Haste and bring
him back.

Exit Sebastian.

FREDERICK.
The colonel's mad, I never saw him thus before. I'll after 'em
lest he do some mischief.

Exit.

Scene xv

The same.

ANGELLICA.
    I am all rage! My first love defeated!
    For such a one who has no other merit
    Than being Don Pedro's sister. Willmore loves her!
    I know 'tis so. He will not see me now, thought oft invited
    And broke his word last night, false, perjured man
    He that but yesterday fought for my favours,
    Must now be hired and courted to my arms.

MORETTA.
    Angellica, I told you what would come on't.
    Why did you give him five hundred crowns, but to set himself
    out for other lovers? You should have kept him poor if you had
    meant to have had any good from him.

ANGELLICA.
    Name not such trifles! Had I given him
    All that my youth has ever earned from sin,
    I had not lost a thought nor sigh upon't,
    But I have given him my virgin heart,
    My virgin heart, Moretta! Oh, 'tis gone!

MORETTA.
    Curse on him, here he comes. How fine you have made him,
    too.

Enter Willmore and Sebastian; Angellica turns and walks away.

WILLMORE.
    How now, turned shadow? Fly when I pursue,
    And follow when I fly?
    (Sings) 'Stay, gentle shadow of my dove,
    And tell me ere I go,
    Whether the substance may not prove
    A fleeting thing like you.'
    As she turns she looks on him.
    There's a soft kind look remaining yet.

ANGELLICA.
    Well, sir, you may be gay. All happiness, all joys pursue you
    still. Fortune's your slave, and gives you every hour choice of
    new hearts and beauties, till you are cloyed with the repeated
    bliss which others vainly languish for. But know, false man,
    that you have done me wrong *(Turns away in rage.)*

WILLMORE.
    Pox o' this whining. My business is to laugh and love. A pox
    on't, I hate your sullen lover. A man shall lose as much time to
    put you in humour now as would serve to gain a new woman.

ANGELLICA.
    I scorn to quench that fire I cannot raise,
    Or do the drudgery of your virtuous mistress.

WILLMORE.
    A virtuous mistress? Why, what the devil should I do with a
    virtuous woman? A sort of ill-natured creatures that take a
    pride to torment a lover. Virtue is but an infirmity in woman.

ANGELLICA.
    I will not answer for your mistress's virtue,
    But I could wish you would persuade my heart
    'Twas her two hundred thousand crowns you courted,
    And not her youth!

WILLMORE.
                      Two hundred thousand crowns!
    What story's this? What trick? What woman, ha!

ANGELLICA.
    How strange you make it.
    Have you forgot the creature you entertained on the Piazza last
    night?

WILLMORE.
    (aside) Ha! My gipsy worth two hundred thousand crowns!
    Oh, how I long to be with her! Pox, I knew she was of quality.

ANGELLICA.
    False man! I see my ruin in thy face.
    How many vows you breathed upon my bosom
    Never to be unjust. Have you forgot so soon?

WILLMORE.
    Faith, no; I was just coming to repeat 'em.

Enter Hellena, dressed in a new guise.

WILLMORE.
    (aside). Would she would be angry again and leave me.

HELLENA.
    Pray, good grave gentlewoman, is not this Angellica?

MORETTA.
    My too young sir, it is.

HELLENA.
    My mad captain's with her too, for all his swearing. How this
    inconstant humour makes me love him! Well something I'll do
    to vex him for this.

MORETTA.
  (To Angellica). Madam, I hope here's one from Don Antonio.

ANGELLICA.
  I will not speak with him. Am I in humour to receive a lover?

WILLMORE.
  Not speak with him? Why, I'll be gone, and wait your idler minutes. Can I show less obedience to the thing I love so fondly? *(Offers to go.)*

ANGELLICA.
  A fine excuse this! Stay –

WILLMORE.
  And hinder your advantage with Antonio? Should I repay your bounties so ungratefully?

ANGELLICA.
  (to Hellena). Come hither, boy. – *(To Willmore.)* That I may let you see,
  How much above the advantages you name
  I prize one minute's joy with you.

WILLMORE.
  (aside). Death, how shall I get away? – Madam,
  'Tis not convenient I stay with you.
  I have a friend – that's dangerously sick.

ANGELLICA.
  I see you're impatient. Yet you shall stay.

WILLMORE.
  (aside). And miss my assignation with my gypsy.

                                                    Moretta exits

HELLENA.
  (to Angellica). Madam,
  You'll hardly pardon my intrusion
  When you shall know my business.
  Alas, I am too young to tell my tale with art;
  But there must be a wondrous store of goodness
  Where so much rare and virgin beauty dwells.

ANGELLICA.
  A pretty advocate, whoever sent thee.
  Prithee proceed.
  (To Willmore, who is stealing off)
              Nay, sir, you shall not go.

WILLMORE.
  (aside). Pox on't, she stays me out of spite.

HELLENA.
  I am related to a lady, madam,
  Young, rich, and nobly born, but has the fate
  To be in love with a young English gentleman.
  Strangely she loves him, at first sight she loved him,
  For he, she said, had charms in every word.

WILLMORE.
  (aside). Ha! Egad, I hope this concerns me.

ANGELLICA.
  (aside). 'Tis my false man he means. Would he were gone.
  This praise will raise his pride, and ruin me.
  (To Willmore) Well, since you are so impatient to be gone,
  I will release you, sir.

WILLMORE.
  (aside). Nay, then I'm sure 'twas me he spoke of – no, Madam,
  I've considered better on't, and will not give you cause of jealousy.

ANGELLICA.
  But sir, I've business that concerns you not.

WILLMORE.
  This shall not do; I know 'tis but to try me.

ANGELLICA.
  Well, to your story, boy. *(Aside)* Though 'twill undo me.

HELLENA.
  With this addition to his other beauties,
  He won her unresisting tender heart.
  Today was the appointed time by both
  To consummate their bliss in holy wedlock.
  And whilst she languished for th'expected bridegroom,
  She heard he paid his broken vows to you.

WILLMORE.
  (aside). So, this is some dear rogue that's in love with me, and this way lets me know it.

ANGELLICA.
  Now I perceive
  The cause of thy impatience to be gone,
  And all the business of this glorious dress.

WILLMORE.
  Damn the young prater; I know not what he means.

HELLENA.
  Madam,
  In your fair eyes I read too much concern
  To tell my farther business.

ANGELLICA.
> Prithee, sweet youth, talk on: thou mayst perhaps
> Raise here a storm that may undo my passion,
> For that I'll grant thee anything.

HELLENA.
> Madam, 'tis to entreat you (oh unreasonable)
> You would not see this stranger, more
> For if you do, she vows you are undone;
> Though nature never made a man so excellent,
> And sure he'd been a god, but for inconstancy.

WILLMORE.
> (*aside*). Ah, rogue, how finely he's instructed! 'Tis plain, some woman that has seen me *en passant*.

ANGELLICA.
> Do you know the man you speak of?

HELLENA.
> Yes, madam, he goes about in buff.

ANGELLICA.
> (*to Willmore*). Thou false as hell, what canst thou say to this?

WILLMORE.
> By heaven –

ANGELLICA.
> Hold, do not damn thyself –

HELLENA.
> Nor hope to be believed.

He walks about; they follow.

ANGELLICA.
> Oh perjured man!
> Is't thus you pay my generous passion back?

HELLENA.
> Why would you, sir, abuse my lady's faith?

ANGELLICA.
> And use me so unhumanly.

HELLENA.
> A maid so young, so innocent –

WILLMORE.
> Ah, young devil.

ANGELLICA.
> Dost thou not know thy life is in my power?

HELLENA.
> Or think my lady cannot be revenged?

WILLMORE.
> (*aside*). So, so, the storm comes finely on.

ANGELLICA.
> Now thou art silent: guilt has struck thee dumb.
> Oh, hadst thou still been so, I'd lived in safety.

She turns away and weeps.

WILLMORE.
> (*aside to Hellena*). Sweetheart, the lady's name and house – quickly! I'm impatient to be with her.

Looks toward Angellica to watch her turning, and as she comes towards them he meets her.

HELLENA.
> (*aside*). So, now is he for another woman.

WILLMORE.
> The impudent'st young thing in nature: I cannot persuade him out of his error, madam.

ANGELLICA.
> I know he's in the right; yet thou'st a tongue
> That would persuade him to deny his faith.

In rage walks away.

WILLMORE.
> (*said softly to Hellena*). Her name, dear boy, her name!

HELLENA.
> Have you forgot it, sir?

WILLMORE.
> (*aside*). Oh, I perceive he's not to know
> I am a stranger to his lady.
> – Yes, yes, I do know, but I have forgot the –
> (*Angellica turns.*) – By heaven, such early confidence I never saw.

ANGELLICA.
> Did I not charge you with this mistress, sir?
> Which you denied, though I beheld your perjury.
> This little generosity of thine has rendered back my heart.

WILLMORE.
> (*to Hellena*). So, you have made sweet work here, my little mischief. Look to't your lady be kind and good-natured now, or I shall have but a cursed bargain on't.

Angellica turns toward them.

The rogue's bred up to mischief; art thou so great a fool to credit him?

ANGELLICA.

Yes, I do, and you in vain impose upon me.

Boy. Is not this he you spake of?

HELLENA.

I think it is. I cannot swear, but I vow he has just such another lying lover's look.

Hellena looks in his face; he gazes on her.

WILLMORE.

(*aside*). Ha! Do I not know that face? By heaven, my little gypsy! What a dull dog was I: had I but looked that way I'd known her. Are all my hopes of a new woman banished?

– Egad, if I do not fit thee for this, hang me. (*To Angellica*) Madam, I have found out the plot.

HELLENA.

(*aside*). Oh lord, what does he say? Am I discovered now?

WILLMORE.

Do you see this young spark here?

HELLENA.

(*aside*). He'll tell her who I am.

WILLMORE.

Who do you think this is?

HELLENA.

(*aside*). Ay, ay, he does know me. – Nay, dear captain, I am undone if you discover me.

WILLMORE.

Nay, nay, no cogging; she shall know what a precious mistress I have.

HELLENA.

Will you be such a devil?

WILLMORE.

Nay, nay, I'll teach you to spoil sport you will not make.

– This small ambassador comes not from a person of quality, as you imagine and he says, but from a very errant gypsy: the talking'st, prating'st, canting'st little animal thou ever saw'st.

ANGELLICA.

This news you tell me, that's the thing I mean.

HELLENA.

(*aside*). Would I were well off the place! If ever I go a-captain-hunting again –

WILLMORE.

Mean that thing? That gypsy thing? Thou mayst as well be jealous of thy monkey or parrot, a dream were a better enjoyment – a creature of a constitution fitter for heaven than man.

HELLENA.

(*aside*). Though I'm sure he lies, yet this vexes me.

WILLMORE.

You may return, my little brazen head, and tell your lady, that till she be handsome enough to be beloved, or I dull enough to be religious, there will be small hopes of me.

ANGELLICA.

Did you not promise, then, to marry her?

WILLMORE.

Not I, by heaven

ANGELLICA.

You cannot undeceive my fears and torments, till you have vowed you will marry her.

HELLENA.

(*aside*). If he swears that, he'll be revenged on me indeed for all my rogueries.

WILLMORE.

To satisfy your jealousy I swear –

HELLENA.

Oh, no swearing, dear captain.

WILLMORE.

If it were possible I should ever be inclined to marry, it should be some kind young sinner: one that has generosity enough to give a favour handsomely to one that can ask it discreetly, and one that has wit enought to manage an intrigue of love. Oh, how civil such a wench is to a man that does her the honour to marry her.

ANGELLICA.

By heaven, there's no faith in anything he says.

(*Enter Moretta*)

MORETTA.

Madam, Don Antonio and Don Pedro sue to see thee.

HELLENA.

(*aside*). Ha! Antonio and my brother. They may be coming hither, and they'll certainly discover me. I'll therefore retire without a ceremony.

Exit Hellena.

ANGELLICA.
I'll see Antonio. Get my coach ready.

MORETTA.
Yes, madam.

Moretta goes.

WILLMORE.
Alas, madam, must I be gone and leave you to the enjoyment of my rival?

ANGELLICA.
Dull man, that canst not see how ill, how poor,
That false dissimulation looks. Be gone,
And never let me see thy cozening face again.

WILLMORE.
Farewell, till you're in better humour – *(Aside)* I'm glad of this release. Now where is my gypsy?

Exit Willmore.

ANGELLICA.
Oh, with what willing haste he took his leave,
He's gone, and in this ague of my soul
The shivering fit returns.
In vain I have consulted all my charms,
And thought my eyes could kindle lasting fires,
I had forgot my name, my infamy,
And how all men prefer the younger mistress.
Well, sir, since I am not fit to be beloved,
I am resolved to think on some revenge
On him that shamed me thus.
And made of me a gull and slave at Carnival.

She goes.

Scene xvi

The street.
Enter the three sisters, dressed as nymphs and with long heads of hair.

FLORINDA.
We're happily escaped, and yet I tremble still. Our brother's angry!

VALERIA.
A lover and fear! Why, I am but half an one yet and I have courage for any attempt.

HELLENA.
But why would you have us in new guises?

VALERIA.
Because our brother hath found out our old ones.

FLORINDA.
Prithee, what hadst done with Callis?

VALERIA.
When I saw no reason would do good on her, as she was looking for something in the great chest, I toppled her in by the heels, locked her up, and left her bawling for help.

FLORINDA.
'Tis well you resolve to follow my fortunes, for thou darest never appear at home again after such an action.

VALERIA.
That's according to Frederick and I shall agree. But to our business: I delivered your note to Bevile and I told him of your resolution of making your escape today . . . I bade him seek our brother out and persuade him that all that passed upon the Molo was but a Carnival mirth.

FLORINDA.
Yet I am afraid lest our devices go awry.

VALERIA.
Nay, has not my wit served well till now? How now, Hellena? Silent for this once? Does it go ill with your affairs also?

HELLENA.
I know not yet. Nor know I well how I should handle my mad captain, for he's as hard to catch as a falcon with no tresses.

FLORINDA.
O heavens! Here comes our brother, and Belvile with him too. I muse they are become friends again.

VALERIA.
Up, sisters.

They put up their vizards. Enter Don Pedro and Belvile in serious discourse; Willmore also.

VALERIA.
I'll walk boldly by them, and draw Pedro off lest he suspect you.

BELVILE.
It was a mirth, no more.

PEDRO.
'Tis well, we're friends again.

WILLMORE.
Ha! A woman, and of excellent mien!

PEDRO.
She throws a kind look back on you.

WILLMORE.
Death, 'tis a likely wench, and that kind look shall not be cast away. I'll follow her.

BELVILE.
Prithee do not.

WILLMORE.
Do not? By heavens, to the antipodes, with such an invitation.

She goes out, and Willmore follows her.

BELVILE.
'Tis a mad fellow for a wench.

Enter Frederick.

FREDERICK.
Oh, colonel, such news!

BELVILE.
Prithee what?

FREDERICK.
News that will make you laugh in spite of fortune. Ned Blunt's been cheated, sir, rarely cheated of all but a harlot's drawers.

PEDRO.
Who is't has met with this ill usage, sir?

BELVILE.
A friend of ours whom you must see for mirth's sake –

PEDRO.
What is he?

BELVILE.
An Englishman that yet ne'er knew the want of money, and t'will be a great jest to see how simply he'll look without it. Prithee, Fred, do you go home and keep him in that posture till we come.

Frederick goes.

BELVILE.
(aside). I'll employ Don Pedro in this to give Florinda time for an escape. Sir, let us first dally a little with yonder nymphs. There's one for each.

PEDRO.
Content! I'll venture with the second. Do you Belvile, take the

third. *(Goes after Florinda.)*

Florinda advances from farther end of the scene, looking behind her.

FLORINDA.
Ha, my brother advancing this way. Good heavens defend me from being seen by him.

She goes.

Pedro follows her.

PEDRO.
Nay, be not coy. Here's coin for you.

Follows her. Re-enter Valeria, Willmore following.

WILLMORE.
Ah! There she sails. She looks back as she were willing to be boarded. I'll warrant her prize.

Valeria goes and he follows.

Enter Hellena, just as he goes out.

HELLENA.
Ha, now my captain has Valeria in chase.

She goes.

Pedro following.

PEDRO.
Do I spy you again? Methought I'd lost you. Stay!

He goes, calling after her.

Re-enter Florinda.

FLORINDA.
What shall I do? I fear my brother still pursues me. Ha! here's a door open. I'll venture in. My life and honour are at stake, and my necessity has no choice.

She goes into the Englishmen's lodgings as Valeria enters.

VALERIA.
This is Belvile's lodging. She's gone in as readily as if she know it. Hah, here's that mad fellow again, and my brother too. I dare not venture in yet, but will watch my opportunity.

Goes.

Re-enter Willmore and Pedro from different sides.

WILLMORE.
I have lost her hereabouts.

PEDRO.
I've lost mine too. Let's seek out Belvile.

Hellena enters aside, watching.

WILLMORE.
 Pox on't, she must not escape me so.

 Goes out.

HELLENA.
 Well, there's no checking him in this humour.
 I must devise some newer trick to plague him.

 She goes.

Scene xvii

A chamber.
Enter Blunt

BLUNT.
 A pox on this tailor, for not yet bringing home the clothes I
 bespoke! And a pox of all poor cavaliers! A man can never keep
 a spare suit for 'em, and I shall have these rogues come in and
 find me naked. There's the worst of all – the colonel and
 Willmore, that rogue, will abuse me out of all Christian
 patience. The rascals shall not insult over me too much for I'm
 resolved to arm myself.
   What a dog was I to believe woman, to be thus soothed into a
 cozening. A fine ladylike whore to cheat me thus. A pox light on
 her, I shall never be reconciled to the sex more. What would I
 give her to have one of 'em within my reach now! Any mortal
 thing in petticoats, on whom to be revenged. But, here's a
 cursed book, *A Warning to English Travellers* – this may instruct
 me how to prevent such mischiefs now 'tis too late. O dog. O
 silly dog! Well, 'tis a rare convenient thing to read a little now
 and then to ease the mind.

Sits down and reads. Enter to him Florinda.

FLORINDA.
 This house is haunted, sure. 'Tis well furnished, and no living
 thing inhabits it. Ha! A man! Heavens, how he's attired! Yet I
 must venture now to speak to him. – Sir.

Blunt starts up and gazes.

BLUNT.
 Ha, what's here?

FLORINDA.
 If I may not interrupt your meditations –

BLUNT.
 Are my wishes granted? And is not that a she creature?
 'Adsheartlikins, 'tis – What wretched thing art thou, ha?

FLORINDA.
 A very wretched maid, forced by strange unlucky accident to
 seek a safety here, and must be ruined if you do not grant it.

BLUNT.
 Dost thou know, miserable woman, into what den of mischiefs
 thou art fallen? Dost not see something in my looks that frights
 thy guilty soul?

FLORINDA.
 Alas, what mean you, sir? I beseech you, as you seem a
 gentleman, pity a harmless virgin that takes your house for
 sanctuary.

BLUNT.
 Talk on, talk on; and weep, too. Do, flatter me out of my senses
 again. A harmless virgin with a pox; as much one as t'other.
 'Adsheartlikins, why, what the devil, can I not be safe in my
 chamber from you? Nay, not even being naked too cannot
 secure me? This is an impudence greater than has invaded me
 yet. Come, no resistance! (*pulls her rudely*) To the bed within!

FLORINDA.
 Dare you be so cruel?

BLUNT.
 Cruel? Yes, thou shalt lie with me. Not that I care for the
 enjoyment, but to let thee see I . . . will be revenged on one
 whore for the sins of another . . . I will flatter thee, and beat
 thee; embrace thee and rob thee, as she did me; fawn on thee,
 and strip thee stark naked; then hang thee out at my window by
 the heels, with a paper of scurvy verses fastened to thy breast in
 praise of damnable women. Come, come, along.

Enter Frederick.

FREDERICK.
 Ha, what's here to do?

BLUNT.
 'Adsheartlikins, Fred, I am glad thou art come, to be a witness
 of my dire revenge.

FREDERICK.
 What's this? Another person of quality, who is upon the ramble
 to supply the defects of some grave impotent husband?

BLUNT.
 No, this has another pretence, some very fortunate accident
 brought her hither . . . to fool's haven . . . Is the ass to be cajoled

again, think ye? No, young one, therefore prepare for both my pleasures of enjoyment and revenge. For I am resolved to make up my loss here on thy body . . .

FREDERICK.
Now, mistress, what do you think of this?

FLORINDA.
I think he will not, dares not be so barbarous.

FREDERICK.
Have a care, Blunt, she fetched a deep sigh; she is enamoured with they sword and drawers. I fear she'll strip thee even of that; there are of her calling such unconscionable baggages and such dextrous thieves, they'll flea a man and he shall ne'er miss his skin till he feels the cold. (*Aside*) There was a countryman of ours robbed of a row of teeth whilst he was a-sleeping, which the jilt made him buy again when he waked.

BLUNT.
'Adsheartlikins, why this is most abominable!

FREDERICK.
You see, lady, how little reason we have to trust you.

FLORINDA.
By all that's holy, I am none such. I entered here to save a life in danger.

FREDERICK.
For no goodness, I'll warrant her.

FLORINDA.
I am a lady of quality.

FREDERICK.
Very like! Why go you thus tricked out so wantonly?

FLORINDA.
Why, for 'tis Carnival.

FREDERICK.
Faith, damsel, we are not fellows to be caught twice in the same trap. Look on that wreck, a tight vessel when he set out of haven, and see how a female picaroon of this island of rogues has shattered him.

BLUNT.
'Adsheartlikins, we'll both lie with her, and then let me alone to bang her.

FREDERICK.
I'm ready to serve you in matters of revenge that has a double pleasure in't.

BLUNT.
Well said – You hear, little one, how you are condemned by public vote to lie with us.

FREDERICK.
There's no resisting your destiny, sweetheart. (*Pulls her.*)

FLORINDA.
Stay, sir, I have seen you with Belvile, an English cavalier. For this sake, use me kindly. You know him, sir.

FREDERICK.
Belvile?

BLUNT.
Belvile? Why yes, sweeting, we do know Belvile, and wish he were with us now. He's a cormorant at whore and bacon. He'd have a limb or two of thee, my virgin pullet . . .

FLORINDA.
Sir, if you have any esteem for that Belvile, I conjure you to treat me with more gentleness . . .

FREDERICK.
Hark'ee, Blunt, I doubt we are mistaken in this matter.

FLORINDA.
Sir, if you find me not worth Belvile's care, use me as you please. And that you may think I merit better treatment than you threaten, pray take this present.

Gives him a ring. He looks on it.

BLUNT.
Hum, a diamond!

FREDERICK.
I begin to suspect something, and 'twould anger us vilely to be trussed up for a rape upon a maid of quality, when we only believe we ruffle a harlot.

BLUNT.
Thou art a credulous fellow. Why, my saint prattled as parlously as this does . . .

FREDERICK.
Yet let this ring reprieve her till we see Belvile.

BLUNT.
That's hard, yet I will grant it.

Enter Philip.

PHILIP.
Oh, sir, the colonel is just come in with Willmore and a Spaniard of quality, and talks of having you to dinner with 'em.

But the tailor's not yet come.

BLUNT.

'Adsheartlikins, I'm undone! You, sirrah, upon your life, say I am not at home, or that I'm asleep, or – or anything, Away.

Philip goes.

Hark'ee, Fred, lock up the wench in your chamber.

FREDERICK.

Fear nothing, madam: whate'er he threatens, you are safe whilst in my hands.

Exeunt Frederick and Florinda.

Scene xviii

The same.
A great knocking as at the chamber door.

VOICES.

(call within). Ned! Ned Blunt! Ned Blunt!

PHILIP.

(within). Why, he's dead, sir, he has not been seen today.

BELVILE.

Willmore. Let's break open the door.

BLUNT.

'Adsheartlikins. Ha, break open the door?

A great noise within, at the door again.

BLUNT.

– Hold, hold! What do you mean, gentleman, what do you mean?

BELVILE.

(within). Oh, rogue, art alive? Prithee open the door and convince us.

BLUNT.

No, no, no, no, gentlemen . . . I am at my devotion. 'Adsheartlikins, will you not allow a man time to pray?

BLUNT.

(within). Turned religious? A greater wonder than the first! Therefore open quickly . . .

BLUNT.

Why hark'ee, colonel, to tell the truth, I have a wench with me. You apprehend me?

WILLMORE.

(within). How, a wench? Nay then, we must enter and partake also. Come, come, lend's more hands to the door. Now heave, all together. *(Breaks open the door.)* So, well done, my boys.

Enter Belvile, Willmore, and Pedro. Blunt looks simply, they all laugh at him; he lays his hand on his sword.

BLUNT.

Hark'ee sirs, laugh out your laugh quickly, d'ye hear, and be gone. I shall spoil your sport else, I shall . . . *(Aside)* 'Adsheartlikins, a plague upon my tailor!

WILLMORE.

'Sdeath, how the whore has dressed him! Faith, sir, I'm sorry.

BLUNT.

Are you so, sir? Keep't to yourself then, sir, I advise you, d'ye hear, for I can as little endure your pity as his mirth.

BLUNT.

Why so peevish, good Ned?

BLUNT.

Look ye settle me a good sober countenance, and that quickly, too, or you shall know Ned Blunt is not –

BELVILE.

Not everybody, we know that.

BLUNT.

Not an ass to be laughed at, sir.

PEDRO.

Sir, though I'm a stranger to you, I am ashamed at the rudeness of my nation; and could you learn who did it, would assist you to make an example of 'em.

BLUNT.

Why ay, there's one speaks sense now, and handsomely. And let me tell you, gentlemen, I should not have showed myself like a jack pudding thus to have made you mirth, but that I have revenge within my power. For know, I have got into my possession a female, who had better have fallen under any curse than the ruin I design her. 'Adsheartlikins, she assaulted me here in my own chamber, and had doubtless committed a rape upon me, had not this sword defended me.

FREDERICK.

(entering). I know not that, but o' my conscience thou had ravished her, had she not redeemed herself with a ring. Let's see't, Blunt.

Blunt shows the ring.

BELVILE.

(aside). Ha! The ring I gave Florinda when we exchanged our vows! – Hark'ee, Blunt – (Goes to whisper to him.)

WILLMORE.

No whispering, good colonel, there's a woman in the case. No whispering.

BELVILE.

(aside to Blunt). Hark'ee, fool, be advised, and conceal both the ring and the story for your reputation's sake. Do not let people know what despised cullies we English are.

WILLMORE.

Come, come. We'll see her; let her be what she will, we'll see her.

PEDRO.

Ay, ay, let us see her. I can soon discover whether she be of quality, or for your diversion.

BLUNT.

She's in Fred's custody.

WILLMORE.

Come, come the key –

To Frederick, who gives him the key. They are going.

BELVILE.

– Stay, gentlemen! (Aside) Yet if I hinder 'em, they shall discover all – Hold, let's go one at once. Give me the key.

WILLMORE.

Nay, hold there, colonel, I'll go first.

FREDERICK.

Nay, no dispute, Ned and I have the propriety of her.

WILLMORE.

Damn propriety! Then we'll draw cuts. (Belvile goes to whisper to Willmore.) Nay, no corruption, good colonel. Come, the longest sword carries her.

They all draw, forgetting Don Pedro being a Spaniard, had the longest.

BLUNT.

I yield up my interest to you, sir, and that will be revenge sufficient.

WILLMORE.

(Aside) Pox of his Toledo, I had forgot that. (To Pedro) The wench is yours.

FREDERICK.

Come, sir, I'll conduct you to the lady.

BELVILE.

(aside). To hinder him will certainly discover her.

PEDRO.

Lady, sure 'tis some common carrion. She'd never haunt your house else.

Exit Pedro.

BELVILE.

– Dost know, dull beast, what mischief thou hast done?

Willmore walking up and down, out of humour.

WILLMORE.

Ay, ay, to trust our fortune to lots! A devil on't, 'twas madness.

BELVILE.

Oh, intolerable sot –

PEDRO

(off). 'Tis a hot, crafty, queen, she is so eager to go to it. I'll have her.

Florinda runs in pursued by Pedro.

FLORINDA.

(aside). Good heaven defend me from discovery!

PEDRO.

'Tis but in vain to fly me; you're fallen to my lot . . .

BELVILE.

(aside) Sure she's undiscovered yet but how shall I bring her off?

WILLMORE.

(aside). Why, what a pox, is not this my woman, the same I followed but now?

Pedro talking to Florinda, who walks up and down.

PEDRO.

As if I did not know ye, and your business here.

FLORINDA.

(aside). Good heaven, I fear he does indeed.

PEDRO.

Come, what bashful? Be you as kind as I know you meant to be when you entered here. S'life, she's goodly limbed. I'll have her.

WILLMORE.

But sir, perhaps the lady will not be imposed upon. Let her choose her man.

PEDRO.

Yea, I am better bred than not to leave her choice free. Come mistress, leave off this pretended coyness and take your pick of five good fellows that are as eager for the act thou camest for as thou art apt to undergo it. Or if you will, take all of us and let me be first i' the file.

Enter Valeria, and is surprised at the sight of Don Pedro.

VALERIA.

Hold!

FLORINDA. ⎱
PEDRO.   ⎰   Valeria!
FREDERICK. ⎰

FREDERICK.

My little gypsy!

VALERIA

(*aside*). Don Pedro! There's no avoiding him. (*to Pedro*). Oh, I have found you, sir! The strangest accident – if I had breath – to tell it.

PEDRO.

Speak! Is Florinda safe? Hellena well?

VALERIA.

Ay, ay, sir. Florinda is safe – (*Aside*) From any fears of you.

PEDRO.

Why, where's Florinda? Speak!

VALERIA.

Ay, where indeed, sir; I wish I could inform you. But to hold you no longer in doubt –

FLORINDA.

(*Aside*). Oh what will she say?

VALERIA.

She's fled away in the habit – of one of her pages, sir. But Callis thinks you may retrieve her yet, if you make haste away. She'll tell you, sir, the rest . . . (*Aside*) If you can find her out.

PEDRO.

Dishonourable girl, she has undone my aim – (*To Belvile*) Sir, you see my necessity of leaving you, and I hope you'll pardon it. My sister, I know, will make her flight to you; and if she do, I shall expect she should be rendered back.

BELVILE.

I shall consult my love and honour, sir.

Exit Pedro.

FLORINDA.

(*to Valeria*). My dear preserver, let me embrace thee.

WILLMORE.

What the devil's all this?

BLUNT.

Mystery, by this light.

VALERIA.

Come, come, make haste and get yourselves married quickly, for our brother will return again.

BELVILE.

I'm so surprised with fears and joys, I can scarce persuade my heart into a faith of what I see.

WILLMORE.

Hark'ee colonel, is this the mistress who has cost you so many sighs, and me so many quarrels with you?

BELVILE.

It is. (*To Florinda*) Pray give him the honour of your hand.

WILLMORE.

(*kneels and kisses her hand*) . . . Give me your pardon, too.

FLORINDA.

The friend to Belvile may command me anything.

WILLMORE.

(*aside*). Death, would I might; 'tis a surprising beauty.

Enter Philip.

BELVILE.

Philip, run and fetch a father instantly.

Exit Philip.

BLUNT.

(*to Florinda*). I have a pardon to beg, too; but 'adsheartlikins, I am so out of countenance that I'm a dog if I can say anything to purpose.

FLORINDA.

Sir, I heartily forgive you all.

BLUNT.

That's nobly said, sweet lady. – Belvile, prithee present her her ring again, for I find I have not courage to approach her myself. (*Gives him the ring; he gives it to Florinda.*)

FREDERICK.
So, now do I stand like a dog, and have not a syllable to plead my own cause with. By this hand, madam, I was never so thoroughly confounded before, nor shall I ever more dare look up with confidence, till you are pleased to pardon me.

FLORINDA.
Sir, I'll be reconciled to you on one condition; that you'll follow the example of your friend in marrying a maid that does not hate you, and whose fortune, I believe, will not be unwelcome to you.

FREDERICK.
Madam, had I no inclinations that way and if she'll have me, I should obey your kind commands.

BELVILE.
Who, Fred marry? He has few inclinations towards wedlock.

FREDERICK.
Oh, I do not use to boast of my intrigues.

BELVILE.
Boast! Why thou dost nothing but boast.

FREDERICK.
I wish this lady would think me more modest a man.

VALERIA.
She would be sorry then, and not like you half so well. And I should be loath to break my word with you, which was, that if your friend and mine agreed, it should be a match between you and I. (*She gives him her hand.*)

FREDERICK.
Bear witness, colonel, 'tis a bargain. (*Kisses her hand.*)

Enter Philip.

PHILIP.
Sir, I have brought the father that you sent for. He would know your purposes and craves you speak to him; for I know not why you sent for him, nor whether 'twas for a christening or a burying.

Exit Philip.

BELVILE.
'Tis well. And now, my dear Florinda, let's fly to complete that mighty joy we have so long wished and sighed for. – Come Fred, you'll follow?

FREDERICK.
Your example, sir, 'twas ever my ambition in war, and must be so in love.

WILLMORE.
And must not I see this juggling knot tied?

ALL.
No.

BELVILE.
No, thou shalt do us better service and be our guard, lest Don Pedro's sudden return interrupt the ceremony.

WILLMORE.
Content; I'll secure this pass.

Exeunt Belvile, Florinda, Frederick and Valeria.

Re-enter Philip.

PHILIP.
(*to Blunt*). Sir, your tailor waits you in your chamber with a noble suit of clothes all made to your measures. I warrant 'tis a goodly.

BLUNT.
Some comfort yet: I shall not dance naked at the wedding.

Exit Blunt.

PHILIP.
(*to Willmore*). Sir, there's a lady without would speak to you. She's very fine, fair and eager too. I told her you were not at liberty.

WILLMORE.
Nay, bring her in; I dare not quit my post. This can be none but my pretty gypsy.

Exit Philip.

Scene xix

Enter Angellica in a masking habit and vizard. Willmore runs to her.

WILLMORE.
(*to Angellica*). I see you can follow as well as fly. Come, confess thyself the most malicious devil in nature; you think you have done my business with Angellica –

ANGELLICA.
It is not done.

She draws a pistol and holds it to his breast.

WILLMORE.
Ha, 'tis not she! What art thou?

ANGELLICA.
One thou hast injured, and who comes to kill thee for't.

WILLMORE.
Prithee on what acquaintance? For I know thee not.

ANGELLICA.
Behold this face so lost to thy remembrance.

WILLMORE.
Angellica!

ANGELLICA.
Yes, traitor! Does not thy guilty blood run shivering through thy veins?

WILLMORE.
Faith, no child. My blood keeps its old ebbs and flows still, and that usual heat too, that could oblige thee with a kindness, had I but opportunity.

ANGELLICA.
Devil! Dost wanton with my pain?

WILLMORE.
Hold, dear virago! Hold thy hand a little,
I am not now at leisure to be killed.
(*Aside.*) Death, I think she's in earnest.

ANGELLICA.
What have you, sir, to say? –
Nay, do not speak
(*Aside, turning from him*)
For I know well if I should hear thee out,
Thoud'st talk away all that is brave about me
And I have vowed thy death by all that's sacred.

Follows him with the pistol to his breast.

WILLMORE.
Why then, there's an end of a proper handsome fellow,
That might 'a lived to have done good service yet.
That's all I can say to it.

ANGELLICA.
(*pausingly*). Yet – I would give thee time for – penitence.

WILLMORE.
Faith, child, I thank God I have ever took care to lead a good, sober, hopeful life, and am of a religion that teaches me to believe that I shall depart in peace.

ANGELLICA.
Nay, Willmore, tell me first . . . tell me how many
Such poor believing fools thou hast undone?

How many hearts thou hast betrayed to ruin?

WILLMORE.
Why, as I think, no more nor less than you.

ANGELLICA.
You said you loved me.

WILLMORE.
So I did, that instant.

ANGELLICA.
And at that instant I gave you my heart.
I'd price enough and love enough to think
That it could raise thy soul above the vulgar,
Nay, make you all soul too, and soft and constant.
Why did you lie and cheapen me? Alas,
I thought all men were born to be my slaves,
And wore my power like lightning in my eyes;
But when love held the mirror, that cruel glass
Reflected all the weakness of my soul;
My pride was turned to a submissive passion
And so I bowed, which I ne'er did before
To anyone or anything but heaven.
I thought that I had won you and that you
Would value me the higher for my folly.
But now I see you gave me no more than dog lust,
Made me your spaniel bitch; and so I fell
Like a long-worshipped idol at the last
Perceived a fraud, a cheat, a bauble. Why
Didst thou destroy my too long fancied power?
Why didst thou give me oaths? Why didst thou kneel
And make me soft? Why, why didst thou enslave me?

WILLMORE.
Egad, I see thy heart is shrewdly nipped.

ANGELLICA.
Ah, sir, ah, sir, I yet had been content
To wear my chains with vanity and joy,
Hadst thou not broke those vows that put them on.

WILLMORE.
Broke my vows? Why, where hast thou lived? Amongst the gods? For I never heard of mortal man that has not broke a thousand vows.

ANGELLICA.
Oh, impudence!

WILLMORE.
Angellica, that beauty has been too long tempting, not to have made a thousand lovers languish, who, in the amorous fever, no

doubt have sworn like me. Did they all die in that faith, still adoring? I do not think they did.

ANGELLICA.
Had I repaid their vows, as I did thine
I would have killed them also that had spurned me.

WILLMORE.
This old general has quite spoiled thee: nothing makes a woman so vain as being flattered. Your old lover ever supplies the defects of age with intolerable dotage, vast charge, and that which you call constancy; and attributing all this to your own merits, you domineer, and throw your favours in's teeth, upbraiding him still with the defects of age, and cuckold him as often as he deceives your expectations.

ANGELLICA.
All this is true, for which I hate thee more.

WILLMORE.
I wish I were that dull, that constant thing
Which thou wouldst have, and nature never meant me.
I must, like cheerful birds, sing in all groves,
And perch a little while on every bough
Billing the next kind she that flies to meet me;
Yet, after all, could build my nest with thee,
Thither repairing when I'd loved my round,
And still reserve a tributary flame.

ANGELLICA.
Willmore, you have a charm almost persuades
Me to take you as you are, and not as I
Will have you be. And yet by god, I will not
Share you with any. I am one that would have
All or none. Therefore, prepare –

WILLMORE.
Sure –

ANGELLICA.
Damn thee! I've heard thee talk too long.

Scene xx

Enter Don Antonio, his arm in a scarf, and lays hold on the pistol.

ANTONIO.
Ha! Angellica!

ANGELLICA.
Antonio! What devil brought thee hither?

ANTONIO.
Love and curiosity, seeing your coach at the door. Let me disarm you of this unbecoming instrument of death. *(Takes away the pistol.)* Amongst the number of your slaves was there not one worthy the honour to have fought your quarrel? – *(To Willmore)* Who are you sir, that are so very wretched to merit death from her?

WILLMORE.
One, sir, that could have made a better end of an amorous quarrel without you, than with you.

ANTONIO.
Sure 'tis the English rogue that took down her picture yesterday; yea, the very same that set on me last night! Blessed opportunity – *(Offers to shoot him.)*

ANGELLICA.
Hold, you're mistaken, sir.

ANTONIO.
By heaven, the very same! What pretensions have you to this lady.

WILLMORE.
Sir, I do not use to be examined, and am ill at all disputes but this – *(Draws; Antonio offers to shoot.)*

ANGELLICA
(To Willmore). Oh, hold! You see he's armed with certain death
And you, Antonio, I command you hold
By all the passion you've so lately vowed me!

ANTONIO.
May you destroy me with your mortal hate
When I refuse obedience to your will.
By all that's holy, I adore you so,
That even my rival, who has charms enough
To make him fall a victim to my jealousy,
Shall live and shall have leave to love on still.

ANGELLICA.
Antonio, yesterday
I'd not have sold my interest in his heart
For all thy sword has won and lost in battle.
(To Willmore)
But now, to show my utmost of contempt,
I give thee life; which, if thou wouldst preserve,
Live where my eyes may never see thee more.

Live to undo someone whose soul may prove
So bravely constant to revenge my love.

(To Antonio)

Sir, since I have a thousand crowns of you,
Come to my chamber; when you will, I care not.

Goes out.

ANTONIO.

Now I have her, St. Jago I am happy.

Antonio follows. Enter Pedro.

PEDRO.

Antonio, stay! Have you forgot Florinda?

ANTONIO.

Don Pedro!

PEDRO.

What coward fear was 't that prevented thee
From meeting me this morning on the Molo?

ANTONIO.

Meet thee?

PEDRO.

Yes, me, I was the man that dared thee.

ANTONIO.

(laughs). Finding myself unapt to use a sword
I send another blade to do thee right.

PEDRO.

But 'twas Florinda's quarrel that we fought.
And you, to show how little you esteemed her
Sent me your rival, Belvile in your place.
When I meet you fit for the dispute,
I'll tell you my resentment.

ANTONIO.

I shall be ready, sir, ere long, to do you reason.

Exit Antonio.

PEDRO.

If I could find Florinda, now whilst my anger's high, I think I
should be kind, and give her to Belvile in revenge.

WILLMORE.

Faith, sir, I know not what you would do, I believe the priest
within has been so kind.

PEDRO.

How? My sister married?

WILLMORE.

I hope by this time she is, and bedded too, or he has not my
longings about him.

PEDRO.

Dares he do this? Does he not fear my power?

WILLMORE.

Faith, not at all; if you will go in and thank him for the favour he
has done your sister, so; if not I have a damned surly crew here
that will keep you till the next tide, and then clap you on board
for prize. My ship lies but a league off the Molo, and we shall
show your donship a damned English rover's trick.

They draw.

BELVILE.

(Off). This rogue's in some new mischief. Ha! Pedro returned!

PEDRO.

Colonel Belvile, I hear you have married my sister.

BELVILE.

You have heard truth then, sir.

PEDRO.

Have I so? Then, sir I wish you joy.

BELVILE.

How?

PEDRO.

By this embrace I do, and I am glad on't.

BELVILE.

Are you in earnest?

PEDRO.

By our long friendship and my obligations to thee, I am. I love
my sister and shall with all honour endeavour to make her
happy. You are fitter for her than Antonio. Come, brother, lead
me to my sister, that she may know I now approve her choice.

Exit Belvile with Pedro.

Scene xxi

Enter Hellena, in the habit of a cabin boy.

WILLMORE.

Ha! My gypsy! Blessings on you for this kindness. Egad child, I
was e'en in despair of ever seeing thee again; my friends are all
provided for within, each man his kind woman. I was e'en

resolved to go abroad, and condemn myself to a lone cabin, and the thoughts of thee.

HELLENA.
And could you have left me behind?

WILLMORE.
Why, 'twould have broke my heart, child.

HELLENA.
Sir, since your friends and mine are all provided for, will you be a faithful friend to me now? If a maid should trust you?

WILLMORE.
For being a friend I cannot promise: thou art of a form so excellent, a face and humour too good for cold, dull friendship. I am parlously afraid of being in love, child, and you have not forgotten how severely you have used me?

HELLENA.
That's all one; such usage you must still look for; to find out all your haunts, to rail at you before all that love you, till I have made you love only me in your own defence, because nobody else will love you.

WILLMORE.
But hast thou no better quality to recommend thyself by?

HELLENA.
Faith none, Captain. I am a love-child a kind of orphan lover, and why I should die a maid, and in a captain's hands too, I do not understand.

WILLMORE.
Egad, I was never clawed away with such broadsides from any female before. Thou hast one virtue I adore – good nature.

HELLENA.
Nay, then, let's lose no time –

WILLMORE.
My time's as precious to me as thine can be. Therefore, dear creature, since we are so well agreed, let's retire to my cabin. Come, my bed's prepared for such a guest all clean and sweet as they fair self. Come, let's retire and fall to.

HELLENA.
'Tis but getting my consent, and the business is soon done. Let but old gaffer Hymen and his priest say amen to't, and I dare lay my mother's daughter by as proper a fellow as your father's son, without fear or blushing.

WILLMORE.
Hold, hold, no bug words, child. Priest and Hymen? No, no,

we'll have no vows but love, child. Marriage is as certain a bane to love as lending money is to friendship. I'll neither ask nor give another vow, though I could be content to have the pleasure of working that great miracle of making a maid a mother, if you durst venture.

HELLENA.
And what shall I get? A cradle full of noise and mischief, with a pack of repentance at my back? Can you teach me to weave swaddling clothes to pass my time with?

WILLMORE.
I can teach thee to weave a true love's knot better.

HELLENA.
So can my dog.

WILLMORE.
Well, I see we are both upon our guards, and I see there's no way to conquer good nature but by yielding. Here, give me thy hand: one kiss, and I am thine.

HELLENA.
One kiss! I am resolved you shall have none, for asking such a sneaking sum. Good friend single-kiss, is all your talking come to this? A kiss, a caudle! I'll to my nunnery. Farewell, captain single-kiss.

Going out. He stays her.

WILLMORE.
By heaven, since we are met again both the Indies shall not buy thee from me. I adore thy nature and will marry thee, and we are so of one humour it must be a bargain. Give me thy hand. *(Kisses her hand.)* And now let the blind ones, love and fortune, do their worst.

HELLENA.
Why, god-a-mercy, captain! Now I beseech you, your name, that I might know at whom to throw my blessings at?

WILLMORE.
I am called Robert – The Constant.

HELLENA.
A very fine name!

WILLMORE.
I hope you have a better.

HELLENA.
I am called Hellena – The Inconstant.

Scene xxii

Enter Pedro, Belvile, Florinda, Frederick and Valeria.

PEDRO.
Ha! Hellena!

FLORINDA.
Hellena!

HELLENA.
Ha! My brother! Now, captain, show your love and courage; stand to your arms and defend me bravely, or I am lost forever.

PEDRO.
What's your business? Speak!

WILLMORE.
Hold off, sir; you have leave to parley only.

HELLENA.
Faith, brother, my business is the same as all living creatures of my age: to love and beloved – and here's the man.

PEDRO.
Hast thou deceived me too; deceived thyself and heaven?

HELLENA.
Be you but kind, let me alone with heaven.

PEDRO.
Belvile, I did not expect this false play from you. Was't not enough you'd gain Florinda, which I pardoned, but your lewd friends too must be enriched with the spoils of a noble family?*(Sees Valeria with Frederick.)* All three ruined in an instant?

BELVILE.
Faith, sir I am as much surprised at this as you can be. Yet, sir, my friends are gentlemen, and ought to be esteemed for their misfortunes, since they have the glory to suffer with the best of men and kings. 'Tis true, he's a rover of fortune, yet a prince aboard his little wooden world.

PEDRO.
(To Willmore) Sir, can you maintain a woman of Hellena's birth and fortune?

WILLMORE.
Faith, sir, I can boast of nothing but a sword which does me right where'er I come and since I loved her before I either knew her birth or name, I must pursue my resolution and marry her.

PEDRO.
And is all your holy intent of becoming a nun debauched into a desire of man?

HELLENA.
Why, I have considered the matter, brother, and find the three hundred thousand crowns my uncle left me, and you cannot keep from me, will be better laid out in love than in religion.

BELVILE.
Let most voices carry it; for heaven or the captain?

FLORINDA.
The captain.

VALERIA.
The captain.

HELLENA.
The captain! Look ye, sir, 'tis a clear case.

PEDRO.
Oh, I am mad! – *(Aside)* If I refuse, my life's in danger – Take her: I shall now be free from fears of her honour. Guard it you now, if you can.

Gives her to him.

WILLMORE.
Faith, sir I am of a nation that are of the opinion a woman's honour is not worth guarding when she has a mind to part with it.

HELLENA.
Well said, captain.

PEDRO.
(to Valeria). This was your plot, Valeria . . .

VALERIA.
There's no altering destiny, sir.

PEDRO.
Sooner than a woman's will. Therefore I forgive you all, and wish you may get my father's pardon as easily, which I fear.

Enter Blunt dressed in a Restoration habit, looking very ridiculously; Philip adjusting his band.

PHILIP.
'Tis very well, sir, I ne'er saw you look so fine.

BLUNT.
Well, sir! 'Adsheartlikins, I tell you 'tis damnable ill, sir. Good lord! A Spanish habit!

BELVILE.
What's the matter, Ned?

BLUNT.
Pray view me round, and judge. *(Turns round.)*

BELVILE.
I must confess thou art a kind of an odd figure.

BLUNT.
Methinks I look like a bouquet garni stuffed full of fool's flesh.

BELVILE.
Methinks 'tis well, and makes thee look e'en cavalier. Come, sir, settle your face and salute your friends.

BLUNT.
Ha! Sayst thou so, my little rover? *(to Hellena)* Lady, if you be one, give me leave to kiss your hand, and tell you, 'adsheartlikins, for all I look so, I am your humble servant.

Carnival music is heard.

FREDERICK.
Hark! What's this?

PHILIP.
The masqueraders are coming up. Pray, let 'em enter, for they're merry.

Enter Masquers with music and dancing.

BLUNT.
'Adsheartlikins, would 'twere lawful to pull off their false faces, that I might see if my doxy were not amongst 'em.

BELVILE.
Nay, let's have no more banging. *(To the Masquers)* Ladies and gentlemen, since you are come so apropos, you must drink with us ere Lent be come.

WILLMORE.
(To Hellena). Come, we'll to the good man within, who stays to give us a cast of his office. Have you no trembling at the near approach?

HELLENA.
No more than you have in an engagement or a tempest.

WILLMORE.
Egad, thou'rt a brave girl, and I admire thy love and courage.

Willmore and Hellena go in.

BELVILE.
I'll give you all a toast. To the Prince over the water. *(Toast.)* And present friends.

They drink a toast with English music. A bell sounds for the beginning of Lent.

BELVILE.
Lent is come.

FREDERICK.
Pox on't.

BELVILE.
So now each one of you must back to's several occupations.

All shed their Carnival gear, the Masquers all appearing as slaves and such like, and go out singing a working song.

FLORINDA.
And must thou back to the wars?

BELVILE.
                              Yea for a little.

FLORINDA.
Alas.

BELVILE.
Soon shall the King be set upon his throne
Then all in England shall enjoy their own.

FLORINDA.
But let us now no future dangers dread
Than present ventures of the marriage bed.

Exeunt to music of the Restoration.